A Game of Three Halves

The Official Kenny Swain Biography

Brian Beard

Pitch Publishing Ltd
A2 Yeoman Gate
Yeoman Way
Durrington
BN13 3QZ

Email: info@pitchpublishing.co.uk
Web: www.pitchpublishing.co.uk

First published by Pitch Publishing in 2013

A CIP catalogue record for this book is available from the British Library.

ISBN: 978-1908051400

Cover design by Olner Design.
Printed and bound by CPI Group (UK) Ltd, Croydon, CR0 4YY

CONTENTS

Foreword

It is rare in the football world that someone can remain at a level of influence in our national game for 40 years without any significant break. Kenny Swain is one of the few! With four decades of experience as a player, coach, teacher and manager he has made an enormous contribution to our national game. Arguably the custodian of the future of English football – working with the young talent that we provide – he has an enormous responsibility having to nurture and guide the young footballing talent of this nation.

Kenny has never been out of work in football which is an incredible achievement shared by very few in an industry where employment is so volatile. In between managerial posts he would turn up at my door and twice I have appointed him to the role of Director of Football at Thomas Telford School, with the aim of making us the strongest performing football school in England, which many would argue we are, thanks to Kenny's contribution.

He has worked with and for exceptional leaders often regarded amongst the best in football and they have had a potent impact upon his philosophy – Dario Gradi, Dave Sexton, Ron Saunders and the great Brian Clough to name but a few. He therefore has a story or two to tell and I have heard many of them. Sometimes they made me laugh, other times made me think as I learned from the wisdom that they shared with him.

I have lived with him, played football with him, coached with him, watched him play and employed him, and I have enjoyed every single moment. He has much to share with the football fraternity and fittingly these experiences and anecdotes can now be enjoyed by others. Football is so much richer for having Kenny Swain's contribution. You will find the read of *A Game of Three Halves* enjoyable and inspirational.

Sir Kevin Satchwell
Headmaster, Thomas Telford School

Chapter 1

The Early Years

Growing up in post-war Liverpool wasn't very different from the 1930s, according to my parents, except for the obvious alterations from air raids. Not long after the last Luftwaffe attacks there were still bomb sites dotted across the landscape for local kids to enjoy, our own adventure playground. My dad remembers seeing incendiary bombs descending like confetti, swinging beneath parachutes, and how everyone was s******g themselves until they landed somewhere else and the relief and sadness he felt because someone else was out of luck that night. Ironically the last air-raid on the city in 1942 destroyed a house which had been home to Alois Hitler, half-brother to Adolf, and birthplace of the Fuhrer's nephew, William Patrick Hitler.

I was born in Birkenhead but only lived there for 18 months before we moved to a flat in Kirkby. Noel Blake, who works alongside me with England Youth players, keeps giving me stick about my bragging rights as a Scouser but he calls himself a Brummie despite being born in Jamaica.

When my family moved across the Mersey before we settled in Kirkby we actually lived in the Anfield area, in Everton Valley. Our house was in a tenement block and we had the upstairs part of the building (posh people would call them maisonettes). Although very young I remember our time living in the city and going to Major Lester County Primary School. My maternal grandmother lived nearby so we were back where my mum had grown up though my dad originally came from Everton.

They were happy days, carefree times with plenty of bombies, bomb sites, around to play on before the programme of urban regeneration swept them away. I recall regular trips to the shop to buy a briquette, a block of compressed coal dust. It would be wrapped in a sheet of newspaper to carry home where it would keep the fire going for a while.

Life for ordinary people in Liverpool was very similar to how it had been for generations and the humour was, as it always has been, and hopefully always will be, typical. Regularly I would be sent to the butcher's to ask if he had a sheep's head and being told if he says "yes" ask him if he can leave the legs on or, and the butcher was as sharp as any of his customers, when I would ask for some lean chops he would ask, "which way do you want them to lean?"

We stayed in the city until I was five or six years old, when we moved to the vast open spaces of Kirkby New Town and a brand new council flat. Kirkby actually became renowned worldwide a few years later as the setting of the 1960s television police drama *Z Cars*. It was really THE place to be then, a kind of boom town with all kinds of building work because the government seemed to be throwing money at new towns all over the place, particularly the North West.

We were in a good spot and, despite it being a flat, we had a back garden, with enough grass to satisfy modest football requirements. And if numbers swelled beyond the capacity of "Estadio Swain" we backed on to school playing fields where there was more than enough space for our regular 50-a-side games though there was no set number of participants. If there were ten of us we played five-a-side, if 30, 15-a-side and so on. If there was an odd number we played rush back goalie, basically a sweeper who could use his hands.

Those games provided a great early learning experience which doesn't seem to be the case nowadays when there are so many indoor distractions like computer games which mean children are less attracted to playing fields or parks. You had to learn on your feet, literally, and develop skills otherwise you never achieved any self-esteem and that was pretty much how it was playing football as a kid in Liverpool where football was such a passion. We couldn't get enough. We'd play on the playground, before school, after school, at lunchtime and in PE lessons. I remember one time doing a football proficiency test, along similar lines to the cycling proficiency test. And I failed. I was devastated because I always thought I could play football. All my mates passed, which made it worse but to add insult to an already bruised ego some of the numbskulls who never got anywhere near the school team passed. It was a salutary lesson for a young Kenny Swain to watch those lads receiving their proficiency certificates at school assembly. I never retook the test.

Though not Kirkby-born I was most certainly Kirkby-bred and that's where I adopted the Scouse religion that is football and where football embraced me. I was a football nut from a very early age and when I started to play organised football at under-12 level I actually kept a detailed record of matches played. I dutifully recorded all scorers, half-time scores, even opposing teams' colours, in a book. I kept that book going until I was about 15 when all my time seemed to be taken up playing football.

By the time I left junior school for Ruffwood Secondary I was already scoring goals and being noticed and that continued when I went into Year 11. Ruffwood was a very big school at the time. If it wasn't the biggest in the country it wasn't far off with a pupil population around 2,000. If the size of the school was a shock to me I was prepared for the sports facilities as my mother had already gone through the brochure we had been sent ahead of us going there. I couldn't believe it when I saw Ruffwood had 16 tennis courts and remember thinking who the heck needs 16 tennis courts, what's this tennis lark all about. There were four football fields and two rugby pitches but I never did get my head around why there were so many tennis courts and so few football pitches.

Ruffwood was a fantastic school and the head, Alan Barnes, was an inspirational leader leading a very good staff. They were our role models, our mentors, and it was a well disciplined school which nurtured the pupils to make the best of what they had. It was a huge school site and one of the earliest comprehensives with a swimming pool and a theatre as well. Never the less it was a daunting prospect for me to move to such a massive establishment but once I arrived each morning it was straight into a game of football on the playground before lessons.

Football was everything to me. As I entered senior school it was still the actual playing of the game that was important. It wasn't until I reached adolescence that the tribal aspect of football allegiance manifested although I had a pretty good grounding at home because my dad and most of the family were Evertonians. He was in his element in the early 1960s, because Everton were the team of the moment and were league champions in 1962/63. Such was the quality of the football they played the club was often referred to as "The School of Science". Liverpool Football Club under Bill Shankly was only just starting to emerge from the Goodison shadow and how Evertonians revelled in that.

I was in my early teens when I got my first season ticket for Everton and had the best of both worlds as I would play for Ruffwood on a Saturday morning and, every other week, dash off to Goodison Park. If the school team was at home I usually went home to get some dinner but if we were away I would go straight to the match. If that were the case it was a diversion via the chippy and digging the middle out of a bread roll and stuffing chips inside and eating on the hoof.

I was fortunate to play in a bloody good team at Ruffwood, which was renowned in the region for its football. My particular team was assisted in no small measure by the cock of the school, Ray Deegan. He was, let's say, an early developer. He was already shaving, and muscle-bound to boot. De rigueur, for a Saturday morning, was us turning up at the away venue and he'd boot the door down to the opposing team's dressing room and fearlessly declare to the enclosed gathering of quivering young footballers: "Come on, who's the f*****g cock of this school, get him in here." Ray must have believed his own reputation. We certainly did. He was menacing and intimidating, which was quite useful for us as he was our centre-half. On the field I was scoring goals quite regularly and like everyone was football daft. Then in 1966 football daftness hit new heights due to the World Cup matches being held in a city that was football mad anyway.

Kirkby Boys' team had a formidable record and were nationally renowned for quite a long time and I managed to get into the team, or I should more accurately state I got into the squad because I rarely got into the team itself. Two of my team-mates went on to trophy-laden careers at the highest level, Terry McDermott and Dennis Mortimer, and most of the regular first team became professional footballers, which illustrates what strength in depth Kirkby Boys had. We had some "extra" players and I was one of those extra players or, as they say these days, a squad player. We were a close-knit bunch and used to get together away from the football although football was still involved. We used to assemble at our flat on Saturday evenings for our regular Subbuteo events.

In our early teens Subbuteo was all the rage so we formed a league, HQ Casa Swain, where we played the games. We had two or three teams each and each game lasted five or six minutes, because fingers get tired too. Then there were the cup competitions so there was a certain amount of fixture congestion because there was never enough time. I bumped into Terry McDermott recently and the first thing he said to me was "do you remember the Subbuteo evenings, when we were kids?" Playing football and table football satisfied teenage appetites but there was the other aspect of football in a football mad city, the one that splits Liverpool into red and blue.

These days whenever I go to Goodison with my son Tom he's fed up with me pointing out one particular turnstile and telling him over and over how I slept under that turnstile waiting to buy my FA Cup Final ticket in 1968, on a cold April night but that's what we did. If you'd collected enough tokens throughout the season to qualify for a ticket all you had to do was make sure you were first in the queue when they went on sale. And the only way to do that was by kipping in a sleeping bag. I wasn't the only one doing that but because I had missed the 1966 FA Cup Final I was determined it would never happen again. In 1966 my dad only had one ticket for the final and because he hadn't seen Everton at Wembley he used it. He promised I would be seeing them too, very soon. I may have missed out on the 1966 FA Cup Final but in the same year I was mesmerised by the World Cup and enriched by the parts of it that reached Merseyside because Goodison Park, my ground, my club, staged some of the first round matches.

In those days our family summer holiday used to be in Talacre, North Wales. We would be picked up outside our flat by taxi, a huge Humber Sceptre. It would turn up to collect us and the taxi driver would keep the engine running in case, as he put it, "I get me wheels nicked". Mum would herd us all out to the car, laden with suitcases, and off we'd go. But in 1966 my mother decided we would go somewhere different so we headed for the exotic-sounding Bognor Regis, via Lime Street Station, which wasn't.

Normally such a change of holiday location would not have presented a problem but 1966 did because of the World Cup and matches being held in Liverpool. I had already attended one game, Brazil versus Bulgaria which most people remember for two things – the free kicks, typically Brazilian, and the start of the physical assault on Pele that marred the tournament.

That night had a major impact on me, a 14-year-old football fan. There was the quality of the Brazilian play and the disgraceful treatment of the best player in the world but there was something else that emerged from a warm summer evening in Liverpool. Walking down Gwladys Street I couldn't believe the colour brought to my city by the Brazil supporters. Yellow, green, white and blue, everywhere you looked, shirts, scarves, banners, all kinds of apparel. It was carnival time and the impact of diverse cultures which was the soul of Brazilian support has never left me and I guess it galvanised my inherent love of football. It isn't the football that is the attraction of a World Cup for me, it's the colour and the spirit of the people following the tournament, following their team, from all corners of the globe, from all kinds of ethnic groups but united by football. That's what the game can do.

But back to that night outside Goodison and one of those seminal events that stay with you for life. My mate Billy Doyle and I were walking along Gwladys Street and this fellah, a huge Brazilian, slapped me, playfully, on the head. I whirled around, resisting the temptation to smack him back, as you do in Liverpool when someone cuffs you about the head. But he beamed an ear to ear grin at us, asking how we were doing and then asked if we had any tickets. Thinking he was maybe looking for some I replied we were "okay thanks".

Naturally World Cup tickets were scarce but he put his hand in his pocket and said, "here, you have these" and flashed a pair of tickets in front of our faces. We couldn't believe it because he offered us two stand tickets whereas we had terrace tickets. It was the first time I ever went into the Goodison Road Stand. Being a novelty for me I couldn't believe how steep the steps up to the top balcony were and it took my breath away but it was fine by the time we settled in our seats to watch the game.

I also saw Brazil versus Hungary but just as I was really getting into that World Cup we had to set off for Bognor so I missed the later games at Goodison, although I did watch Portugal play North Korea on television when Pak Doo Ik and his mates almost caused THE World Cup upset of all time after taking a 3-0 lead, only for Eusebio to take charge and score four of Portugal's five goals in their amazing comeback.

Of course England were making their way towards a semi-final clash with Portugal and I remember worrying that if England did reach the final I might miss it because our holiday didn't end until the day of the final.

I couldn't believe the timing. We were travelling back home on 30th July, World Cup Final day, England v West Germany. The biggest game in English football history and all I could think of was being cooped up in a railway carriage for hours. What made it worse was having to get a train into London then the Underground to Euston to catch the train to Lime Street. I remember masses of people with their Union Jacks, straw boaters and bowler hats celebrating the imminent start to the game. And there was me s******g myself as the Swain family trekked across London, wondering if I was ever going to get home in time to watch the final. But, as luck would have it, we did make it home just in time for kick-off and the rest is history.

It was a very good year because England winning the Jules Rimet Trophy, to give it the correct name, came after Everton won the FA Cup and Liverpool the Football League title so Liverpool, my city, was the centre of the universe. And the music at the time wasn't bad either. If football was an activity we engaged in at regular intervals the music of Liverpool was a constant. It seemed to blare out everywhere; from speakers above shop doorways, transistor radios, market stalls, fairgrounds and, of course, from the PA system at Goodison, and Anfield (not that I was a regular frequenter, only for Everton away). If you were fortunate enough to own a record player, a Dansette being the most popular, you were a bit special and a favoured member of your peer group, as was my sister Jennifer, because she had one.

The Liverpool sound conquered the world in those days and it was a twin force, synonymous with football, to hear the Beatles, Gerry and the Pacemakers, the Searchers, the Merseybeats et al, on our way to football, on our way back and at a stadium. We Liverpudlians are fiercely proud of our musical heritage. I know that music spread nationwide and worldwide but it was a bit more special to us because it was part of our social fabric. We saw ordinary blokes like the Beatles, Billy J Kramer, Gerry Marsden, and they were just like us, working class kids who had grown up in the city and for me, in my early teens, those lads were only a few years older, showing what could be achieved with drive and ambition and, of course, talent.

Lily, who was to become my wife, actually worked for the official Beatles fan club which was a natural progression from when she and her mates, as did many others, used to miss lunch and run off to watch the lunchtime sessions the Beatles played at the Cavern.

Growing up in 1960s Liverpool was fantastic. As I entered my teens there was so much to do and as I grew older my interests widened. Going to the pub for an underage pint and noticing girls were added to the list of teenage leisure pursuits but it was still football, music, drinking and girls, in that order. But also in the process of growing up I became aware of an increasing level of expectation, not from me but from others, including teachers. What was I going to do with my life, what were my work prospects, what were we going to do for a living? And as those questions were bandied about the usual answer from most of my peers was, "I'm gonna go where you go", with a few "me too" confirmations thrown in for good measure. I had no idea where I was going to go. I applied for a couple of engineering apprenticeships because it was something I was quite good at so seemed the obvious thing to do and a few of my mates were similarly inclined so I decided I would get the necessary grades and go to college. However, if I didn't get a job or didn't like anything I was offered, I would stay on at school and do a couple of years in the sixth form. I needed some kind of familiarity because of the feelings of insecurity I had at that stage of my life and it was easier to stay at school among my social group.

Most of my friends decided upon college or university and naturally we sought advice from those teachers who had guided us through school. There was one particular member of staff who figured prominently, Dave Withey, who was the craft and technology teacher but he also took the football team. Dave was always a source of inspiration for all of us. He was very enthusiastic and used to regale us with tales from his college days and a lot of his pupils were inspired to follow in his footsteps and study design technology and PE.

It seemed the obvious course of action for me as I had already sampled the alternative of trying to pursue a career in football. When I was 15 I had a spell at Bolton Wanderers. This chap came round to our house and told us he had seen me play for Kirkby Boys and as they already had Jimmy Redfern and Chris Duffy on their books Bolton wanted me to join them. I used to travel up to Burnden Park twice a week, Tuesdays and Thursdays, by car, which the club sent to pick the three of us up. I think Bill Ridding was the manager at the time and a young Francis Lee was making all the headlines.

There were a lot of good players at Bolton then and I always felt a little overawed, insecure, and never really felt I was good enough. After a while they decided not to offer me an apprenticeship, as it was in those days, and that was upsetting, particularly for my father, who thought I was heading for a career in professional football. And yet, for my mother it had the opposite effect because she wanted me to go to college and have an education. That failed attempt to become a professional footballer reinforced my decision to stay on at school and do my O Levels and A Levels.

I thoroughly enjoyed my time in the sixth form, studying and playing football for the senior school team. There was a new kind of freedom for me once I knew I wasn't joining Bolton and that enhanced my enjoyment of the game. And because I felt less pressure I was able to concentrate on my examinations and achieved eight O Levels and two A Levels, technical drawing and design technology, exactly what I needed to get into college. The same college Dave Withey had attended, Shoreditch. Dave told me there were three or four colleges I could go to but as soon as he mentioned Shoreditch was the best that was good enough for me and a few others in our group.

We were lucky we had someone like that shaping our future, someone we respected enough to seek advice from. There are so many children out there who are insecure, unsure of what to do and with low self-esteem. They need the belief and confidence of elders, teachers, parents and relatives especially when they reach various crossroads in life.

Football was the epicentre of my teens and I was fortunate to fill a gap in my watching experience when Everton returned to Wembley for the FA Cup Final of 1968. After missing out on Wembley in 1966 I was determined to endure no repeat. Me and my mates camped overnight at Goodison when the tickets went on sale and there was no happier bunch of teenage Evertonians on Merseyside when we left, mission accomplished, with those precious pieces of paper. I can't remember who organised the next phase, travel to London, but it was probably Billy Doyle.

We travelled from Lime Street on an overnight train. In those days it wasn't the two-hour journey it is now. I'd like to say it was an overnight sleeper but that would convey an inaccurate picture of luxury travel. It was overnight and we did get some sleep but that was it.

I remember when we met up at the station there were masses of Everton supporters milling around before piling into antique Pullman coaches. It was a pouring of humanity into long narrow boxes like sardines being crammed into a tin. For me it was a novelty because it was the first time I had been away from home overnight. I had travelled with Kirkby Boys but this was the first time I had flown solo although there were four of us, a first adventure without adult supervision.

We dived into the first available carriage and unlike modern trains the carriages were divided into compartments with a narrow corridor running down one side. Each compartment had two mattress-type benches which billowed clouds of dust whenever anyone sat down and above each of those seats was a luggage rack which looked more like a hammock because of the webbing. They were quite appropriate because with a long journey ahead of us they made for comfortable sleeping. We were fortunate because there was only the four of us in one compartment so it meant two sleeping on the seats and the others cosseted in the hammocks swinging above. Not that we got much sleep, we were too busy having a laugh and speculating on how many we would beat West Brom by.

We got into Euston around 6am so it was daylight and although we were all city lads the city of London was a new experience. Next up we had to negotiate the London Underground to Wembley but that early in the morning there didn't seem to be much point so we made our way to Hyde Park Corner but we ended up in Regent's Park. All that grass and we'd brought a ball with us so what else were we going to do on Cup Final day except play football? We were spotted by someone who took a picture of us kicking around, re-enacting how Everton were going to beat West Brom. We posed for a picture and a few hours later we were splashed across the early edition of the *London Evening Standard*. Naturally a few copies of that newspaper made their way to Liverpool later that day.

When we got to Wembley the whole place was a sea of blue but the game itself wasn't a classic although there were a couple of pieces of football history on the day. Ninety minutes ended scoreless so we had extra time and Albion sent Dennis Clarke on for John Kaye to become the first FA Cup Final substitute. Three minutes into the first period of extra time Jeff Astle broke Everton hearts when he scored, with his weaker left foot, to snatch the trophy to add his name to the select band of players who have scored in every round of the FA Cup.

Of course that mattered little to the Everton players and fans who were totally deflated. I'm not ashamed to admit we were in tears, at least I know I was. It had been such a lovely day and for it to end as it had was totally devastating. It emphasised what football was all about, expectation is a killer. It was a wake-up call of sorts because I had played for a few years fairly successfully, without too much disappointment, and the team I followed was successful so that Cup Final defeat was immense. It was perhaps my first experience of the impact expectation can have when it is unrealised. It was my first taste of a factor that would occur many times during my playing career and something which has been integral to my work with England Youth players over recent years.

Defeat is part and parcel of sport and it's how you cope with it that moulds character. How you bounce back from reversals that inevitably crop up, particularly in football, is perhaps the greatest determinant of how you deal with life. It has been the evolution of how I have managed disappointment and the failure to realise expectation that has shaped the way I have pursued my career, as a player and as a coach. Consequently that has moulded how I approach and deal with expectation surrounding our England youngsters.

When the boys get really down I introduce a reality check. I tell them if they want to be involved in football they have to get used to setbacks. I emphasise the need to realise that what they see on the telly, edited highlights, all the good bits, isn't the reality of the game. There are more disappointments and dashed dreams in football than anything else but there is a positive side. When they do have success those moments are so sweet and intoxicating they need to be savoured because they are fleeting and infrequent.

You quickly realise what you have done that day, enjoying one precise moment in time which cannot last. That is why it's so important to live for that moment because, I'm sorry, the next day it is history. However wonderful the achievement, however meritorious an entry on a CV, because that's what the motivation is, getting successes, it's also important to state that success isn't always about winners. However, I feel, and what I try to impart with England is this, it's all about achievement. It is not just about winning, it cannot be, because in any contest, match, competition or whatever, there can only be one winner but the other side of that equation is the opponent or the opposition. They may be the loser but there is achievement in getting to the stage where they have a chance to be a winner but with that comes the certainty that there will also be a loser. But that must not diminish the positivity of achievement.

One of my managers at the Football Association is Ray Clemence and when his CV is considered he has got a long list of success from his career; trophies, winners' medals and caps, and when you look at people like Ryan Giggs and Paul Scholes plus a myriad others in the game you have to think that they are just the tip of the iceberg. The vast majority are achieving all the time and not necessarily winning and it's not just individuals. When clubs such as Watford climb through the divisions and reach the Premier League and don't quite survive and drop down again but start to consolidate they are actually building the foundation of a solid football club. I quote Watford but there are others I could name like Stoke City. I admire Tony Pulis and Peter Coates for what they have done there and how they maintain the club's progression, and the season after reaching the FA Cup Final they evolved even further by taking the club up another rung on the ladder of achievement and into Europe. But with that achievement comes the burden of expectation and the relevance of that was my first encounter with expectation in the 1968 FA Cup Final. Just six weeks prior to the final Everton smashed West Brom away 6-2. Alan Ball netted four so naturally my expectation at Wembley was more of the same. Although I don't remember much from the game itself I do remember an incident after the match which summed up for me, as a 16-year-old fan and throughout my life in football, the synergy of expectation and achievement.

After the Everton team had climbed the 39 steps to collect their losers' medals the crowd was thinning out as fans made their way home. We hung back so we could savour every moment because we did not know when we might be back for another FA Cup Final. As the Everton players conducted their lap of honour, applauding us as we applauded them, I witnessed Alan Ball, the player I idolised, throw something on to the pitch. On the very turf where he had won the World Cup less than two years earlier I am convinced I saw Alan Ball throw away his FA Cup medal and I wasn't the only one. I think he was such a winner he didn't want a symbol of what he obviously regarded as a reward for losing. Looking back on what I have just written something struck me, more than four decades on, which I never realised before. I referred to the Everton medals as "losers' medals", which is exactly what they were, but they were also runners-up medals. I guess my psychology, and the mindset I utilised as a professional footballer, saw my team as losers, they had lost the Cup Final. It is only on reflection I amended my definition to FA Cup runners-up. Not that bad eh?

What I am trying to say is that you can make a positive out of a negative situation, i.e. losing a contest by regarding participation as an achievement even if it doesn't seem as salubrious an achievement as winning. I suppose the Everton players, or any players on a losing team in a final or a championship, don't regard it as being runners-up, they would regard it as being losers. Professional footballers see such results in black and white terms. You are either a winner or a loser and on reflection I experienced a perfect illustration of achievement against expectation with Nottingham Forest in 1983/84.

Just a few years after back-to-back European Cup wins and a Super Cup triumph a club at which expectation had sky-rocketed sold players who had achieved most of that success but still finished third, behind Liverpool and Southampton. I thought it was a fantastic achievement and so did Cloughie given that he had sold Peter Shilton, Trevor Francis, Viv Anderson and also sold, and bought back, Garry Birtles. Then he assembled a side comprising a few old heads like myself, Ian Bowyer and Paul Hart, a few middle-term players like Birtles, Bryn Gunn and Hans van Breukelen and a sprinkling of talented young players coming through like Peter Davenport, Chris Fairclough, Steve Hodge, Colin Walsh and young Nigel. To finish third with a new team, so quickly, was a hell of an achievement, certainly for me to be chasing a league championship that late in my career. That's why I was so appreciative of the opportunity after winning the title with Villa. To view what we did as an achievement and that appreciation began evolving way back in 1968 when a bunch of teenage Everton fans made the long journey back to Liverpool.

We got back to Lime Street at 11.30pm and were roused from our slumber by shouts and whistles. Good job too because we were that exhausted if we hadn't been woken we would have ended up in Carlisle because the train was just about to pull out having disgorged its complement of disappointed Evertonians. Almost certainly I was as disappointed as the rest but in hindsight it was a seminal moment for me as I started to realise that you could regard participation in something as an achievement and even if you didn't win the prize, at least you were part of the raffle. It was the start of an appreciation that continues to this day and it was something I took into every game I played, from Ruffwood School through to RSC Anderlecht, and beyond.

Chapter 2

Teacher Training and Wycombe

Going to college was a massive change in my life particularly as I chose to go somewhere as far away as London. It was laying down a career path. Having applied for apprenticeships at Otis Elevators and General Electric Motors I then decided I didn't want to go to work at 16 when I could enter the sixth form which was something my parents encouraged.

It was the biggest change in my life at a time when I was passing from being a teenager into young adulthood. I was leaving the comfort zone which had cosseted and protected me and taking the first steps into working life but at that time I didn't recognise I was in fact moving into another comfort zone. Looking back college life was in fact a cushion before the reality of actually earning a living.

College was comfortable with three meals a day, a nice warm room, an endless supply of hot water, football, girls and a Student Union bar. It was great but life as a student wasn't all fun because we did have to work and meet deadlines to meet – the trick was to achieve a balance. There were lectures you had to attend but there were a few that were missed but care needed to be taken to avoid a negative effect on coursework. The environment was something special for someone from Kirkby which was flat with no trees. It was an overspill town and a complete contrast to where I went to college.

Shoreditch was located in leafy Runnymede which is famous for the signing of the Magna Carta, the RAF memorial and the JFK memorial and just a few miles away from Windsor, Eton and the river Thames. As well as being surrounded by history it was semi-rural. Coopers Hill, Englefield Green, was just a beautiful setting, the heart of England or at least the heart of what I thought England stands for. Whenever I walked around the campus at Shoreditch I might just as well have been walking on the moon such was the difference to what I was used to.

The first term, in 1970, was very memorable for the only occasion I went home during term time. It was my one and only trip back to Liverpool, probably because I was a little homesick but I soon got over that. There was so much to do and so many people to do things with. I had a couple of friends and there were a couple of older lads who had gone to Shoreditch from Ruffwood so having half a dozen of us from the same school helped. It was a very social environment and we capitalised to the full and that was helped in no small measure by the change Shoreditch implemented when I first went there. It went co-ed.

Talk about perfect timing. Its reputation as a craft college had been founded on being all male but in my first year the college opened its doors to women. There was of course a reaction akin to rampage, by both sexes. Previously girls would be bussed into our place or we would be bussed out to nearby all-female establishments, for dances and discos. We would bus out for 50p a head and enjoy ourselves until returning, usually worse for wear, in the early hours. Now everything we needed was on-site so college social life was fantastic.

Socialisation is an element of higher education that is sometimes overlooked. We had to socialise, it was almost impossible not to and long may that be the case because it does mould a person, it does mould character and is a very worthwhile life experience because it promotes integration and that is a crucial element a person has to negotiate when they eventually enter the workplace. Socialisation either nurtures what you have naturally or introduces it, either way it is a vital part of growing up, a life experience.

I went to Shoreditch to study design technology and its reputation was renowned but it also had a very good name for sport and was a strong PE establishment. My main subject was design technology but my second main was physical education, although I ended up doing a double main which meant PE was elevated to the level of DT, giving more timetabled time for sport. That meant a gathering of like-minded footballers and led to the college getting bloody good at football and someone at that point must have recognised that I had a certain amount of football ability, but it was something that was never truly tested.

I've already written that with Kirkby Boys I was one of a squad and a not very often used member. It was my first experience of how judgemental football is in that one person might rate you and another may not but what doesn't alter is your ability, only a perception of that ability. When I was with Bolton Wanderers as a schoolboy I harboured dreams of becoming a professional footballer. That was my chance, but when they didn't offer me an apprenticeship it didn't upset me because I wasn't really aware of my ability or potential. I was happy playing football at school but soon had to organise my working future.

At Shoreditch my future was training as a teacher and although I wasn't aware of it at the time the instruction I was getting from my tutors influenced what I was going to do 20 years down the line in management and coaching. The whole ethos of teaching began for me at Shoreditch College and there is a certain symmetry between me as a young adult being taught by grown-ups and my work with the England Youth players where I, as an adult, am teaching and coaching teens who are on the verge of adulthood.

The PE tutors and lecturers were very influential for me and PE teachers in schools generally are believed to have the biggest influence on children because so many play sports. And that sports instruction invariably takes place away from the classroom, which can be constraining, but that enhances the responsibility of being a PE teacher which is something they may not be aware of when they first enter the profession. But as one grows and matures there is a growing realisation of the influence over children and with that comes even greater responsibility to exercise that wisely. The more that influence grows the more responsibility increases.

Kevin Satchwell, now Sir Kevin, was in the year above me at Shoreditch and was president of the college football club. He organised everything that was football related including coaching courses for the FA preliminary badge with Bobby Houghton, who would take Malmo to the 1979 European Cup Final.

During my time at Shoreditch I kept in touch with most of the lads from Ruffwood who had gone on to further education in London including Billy Doyle, whose sister Lily would be my future wife. I already knew Lily but when Billy told me his sister was coming down to London and asked if I could get a couple of tickets for a game I was delighted to oblige. I did and subsequently I would go back to Liverpool some weekends where we would meet up and our relationship developed from there.

My second teaching practice, at Peckham Manor Boys' School, was a torturous time, indeed there were many schools in London with notorious reputations and Peckham Manor was just one of them. The school actually offered me a job, in fact I think they offered everyone a job in those days.

Summers for us students were very long but most of us had to take jobs to supplement meagre grants from the government, even if you were fortunate enough to get a grant. Kevin managed to get me a job working on the roads, on the A5 near Cannock. His dad was Irish and most of the gangs we worked on comprised Irish workers. I would stay with Kevin in Wednesbury, on an estate not that different from the one I came from in Kirkby.

The work was hard but well paid. I think we earned something like £5 a day, cash in hand, although as students we didn't have to pay tax. We worked from Monday to Friday but if we worked Saturday the rate of pay went up and we were paid time-and-a-half, meaning that for Saturday morning we got an extra fiver. When I finished at lunchtime on the Saturday I would hitch-hike home to Liverpool with 30 quid in my pocket or what was left. I spent the rest of the weekend at home before returning to Wednesbury in time for work on Monday.

The main part of our job, which probably made a man of me, was lugging concrete kerbstones around. They were heavy and awkward and if not handled properly you could drop one on yourself and break a leg or someone else's. Almost as awkward, and just as dangerous, were the Kango jackhammers. If you didn't perfect their use you ended up with the whole thing stuck fast in solid concrete which then required massive amounts of effort and back muscle to pull out.

That was how my student summers were filled and almost every night, after work, the whole gang of us would be out drinking all over the place. From seasoned 'navvies' who could drink for Ireland to those of us who were still apprentices perfecting the art of beer drinking.

For three years at college my only real concerns were fun and football and as far as my future was concerned, that was most definitely in teaching. On the football front the college team was fairly successful and on a representative front I played for the South East of England College team against the South West of England side, at Wycombe Wanderers' ground, Loakes Park, with its notorious slope. That ground was instrumental in my life as I was later to play there in a testimonial for Wycombe against a Chelsea side managed by Dave Sexton. Dave played at full-back and was marking me as I was playing on the wing. But it was the inter-college game that sparked a chain of events that would eventually lead to me turning my back on the career I had spent three years preparing for.

As I was coming off the pitch at the end of the college game I was approached by a man who introduced himself as Brian Lee. He was the director of the National Sports Centre at Bisham Abbey but was also the manager of Wycombe Wanderers and he asked me if I would like to play for Wycombe. When I told him I was at college just down the road he said he knew that, adding that he had attended the same college. The fact he was also from Merseyside only added to the irony.

Brian told me the players trained twice a week on Tuesday and Thursday, with matches on a Saturday. I explained that the problem was my exams, which were just around the corner. "No problem," he said, and added that it would be okay if I only trained one day a week, Thursday, and played on Saturday and they would pay me £10 per week. If the team won away from home that was worth another £3, if you won at home it was £2 and an away draw was worth £1. I asked for more information about Wycombe and he told me they were a big club in the Isthmian League, to which I said "the what league?"

I did play for Wycombe but was only there for six or seven weeks to the end of that season. Although it was a brief spell it didn't take long for me to realise it was a very good club and I never realised, until then, that players in non-league football were actually paid, so it was a bit of an eye-opener in more ways than one. It also enhanced my social standing at college as I would go back to Shoreditch on a Saturday night with ten pounds burning a hole in my pocket. Putting that into perspective my grant was only £28 for the whole term, peaking at a high of £35, and in those pre-decimal days you could do a lot of damage in the union bar for a quid so very often the drinks were on me. But, however much we, the college team, drank on a Saturday night, we were always right for playing on Sunday.

What a great time life as a student was. Everything was hunky dory. I was playing football twice a week, training once a week and getting paid to boot. I couldn't believe my luck.

I finished my exams in May/June and my plan was to go home to Liverpool for the summer before heading back to London to take up the teaching post I had secured at a school in Ealing, West London, at Twyford School. But while I was at home I got a letter from Dario Gradi, who was on the coaching staff at Stamford Bridge, saying that Chelsea had seen me play and had been in touch with Brian Lee, spoken to him and as a consequence they would like to invite me down for pre-season training in July for a couple of weeks. They offered to pay for all my travel and accommodation. Dario said it would be valuable experience for me whatever happened and whatever I did in the future. He explained that, like me, he had been at teacher training college, Loughborough in his case. He had a spell as a PE teacher but then he went into football and had been a coach ever since. He went on to play for the England amateur international side and all in all made out a good case for at least giving it a go.

The approach from Chelsea came after Brian Lee told me that a number of clubs had inquired about me – Oxford United, Reading and Chelsea. At that time Chelsea weren't the monster club they were to become but they were very popular. They were many supporters' second team as they had a bit of razzmatazz about them. They were also quite successful and it was only three years after they had won the FA Cup and a couple of years after they lifted the European Cup Winners' Cup and there was me on the brink of joining them.

Dario was reserve team coach at Chelsea and had obviously spoken with Dave Sexton, following the testimonial game, and he was making a fairly convincing case to attract me to the club. Conversely Brian Lee, who I naturally discussed this with, presented a convincing counter argument. He pointed out that I already had a teaching post lined up, a regular job with a steady income, something like £23 a week and Wycombe were prepared to put my money up to £15 a week, plus bonuses. That would mean me almost doubling my money and the prospects were looking good. Brian also made the very good point that I could complete my probationary year, which was a concern for me, and still play for Wycombe.

After much deliberation I decided to accept the offer of a trial with Chelsea and the club put me in digs in Wimbledon where I shared with Clive Walker. After a couple of weeks, during the pre-season training, Dario pulled me to one side and said he was sure Dave Sexton was going to offer me a contract because he felt I had a good chance of making the grade. But my concern, which I expressed to Dario, was that I was due to start teaching just a few weeks later. We were already in August so I told Dario I had some serious thinking to do. He told me I would be a fool to turn it down. But I told him I needed to do my probationary year as a teacher, or waste the three years I had just completed. Dario told me not to worry about that because he felt once I got up and running in professional football I would be fine. He certainly reinforced his view that I would never get a chance like that again.

He was right and very soon afterwards Dave Sexton said Chelsea would offer me a contract. He knew what I would get as a teacher, around £20 to £25 a week, so he said the club would offer me £32 per week. He added he couldn't pay me any more because he had the likes of Ray Wilkins, Gary Stanley and Steve Finnieston et al and he couldn't pay me more than younger established players. He sweetened the offer by indicating Chelsea would review the situation in time and that I would also have all my accommodation and travel expenses paid and I would be able to go home, at Chelsea's expense, four or five times a year. That wasn't all because on top of my weekly salary I would be entitled to other "pro" benefits such as appearance money, 20 or 30 quid a week, and on top of that win bonuses. So all of a sudden, if I was to get into the first team, I was talking about a lot of money, for playing football. So it left me with some serious thinking to do about my future. That night I went around to talk with Dario and he told me straight: "Don't hang around before deciding." He was right and I agreed I might never get such an opportunity again.

I rang the head at the school in Ealing, where I was going, and told him I couldn't take up the post. However much I tried to apologise he was miffed at being left with just a few weeks' notice to find another teacher to fill that job. So I signed for Chelsea and in those days you received a signing-on fee so I was in line for something in the region of £500, paid in instalments over two years, although my contract, initially, was for one year plus a one-year option, which was common then.

The money on offer, not to mention the attraction of becoming a professional footballer and realising the dream held my most lads, was Utopia. Considering my background and where I had come from the opportunity before me was massive, but I did agonise, or maybe that's too strong a word. I did mull everything over for a couple of days. I couldn't really lose. Financially I would be comfortable with Wycombe and teaching, or very comfortable with Chelsea. But there was another factor which was very tempting and might tip the scales towards the former and that was Charles Hughes, he of POMO fame (Position Of Maximum Opportunity). According to Brian, Charlie Hughes told him that I was a certainty to play for the England Amateur side that season but, of course, to do that I would have to remain with Wycombe. On the other hand Dario "guaranteed", and bet me £10, that I would play in the Chelsea first team before the end of that 1973/74 season and we shook on it. I wasn't sure if he was trying to convince me to sign or was simply showing faith in me to assure me that I had something worthwhile. I took the bet. And I took the tenner when I did indeed make my debut on 16th March 1974 at home to Newcastle United.

Chapter 3

Chelsea

Chelsea were THE glamour club in 1973. Show business, razzmatazz and then the football was how it seemed, in that order. I remember, when I first reported for pre-season training with my boots in a Tesco bag, Dario Gradi's response was: "We can't have him walking around with a supermarket bag." It was ironic because I did actually take meticulous care of my footwear in those days.

A friend of mine at Ruffwood, Peter Scott, eventually joined Everton and he once invited me down to Bellfield, the Everton training ground. On the guided tour we ended up in the boot room where he explained that as part of his duties he cleaned the players' boots. Peter had a five-litre can of groundnut oil and explained that after the boots were cleaned with a wire brush, the oil would be poured over the boots and rubbed in as deep as possible. I checked out the boots and couldn't believe how soft they were and thought this was the way to do football boots. It was a long way from how my dad used to clean my boots which basically consisted of slapping on copious amounts of Chelsea dubbin, a well-known brand believe it or not, and buffing them with a cloth. From that day onwards that's how I cleaned my boots, indeed most of the lads at college followed suit. It was a practice I maintained throughout my Chelsea career although the apprentices would clean and polish them but if I wasn't satisfied I would do them again, myself.

Another thought from that July day and my first pre-season training session as a professional footballer was that I never felt any trepidation at what lay ahead. Dario had said it would be good experience for me, fun in fact. There was no pressure because I was going into teaching in a couple of months' time so it was to be an enjoyable experience before starting work. But I quickly realised it was basically a trial at Chelsea.

That first day was memorable in so many ways but perhaps the most striking, as I looked around me, was the profusion of star players: Alan Hudson, Ian Hutchinson, Charlie Cooke, Peter Bonetti, Ron Harris, Marvin Hinton, John Dempsey, Peter Osgood, Tommy Baldwin, Chris Garland, all top players I was watching from the terraces just a few years earlier. The first year at Chelsea reinforced what I had first been aware of at Kirkby Boys about how judgemental football could be. At Chelsea it was a talent-packed squad but players could be in the team one week then out the next and there were different reactions from different people to that situation. On top of that there was dressing-room gossip and I quickly realised what a competitive business I was in and how competitive I would have to be if I was to be part of it.

Initially at Chelsea I was very surprised at how out of condition some of the players looked. That perception was reinforced when I saw one or two of them being physically sick, throwing up as pre-season got underway, but not me. I had spent three weeks back home preparing for the tough regime I knew lay ahead so regular runs were the order of the day. I ran two or three miles, every day, through the streets and parks getting myself in condition. I was determined not to make a show of myself and when I saw some stars retch their breakfast onto the pristine turf of the training ground I was very glad I prepared as I did and found I was in fairly good nick.

I always prided myself on being fit but it was a couple of massive steps up from what I was used to when I joined Chelsea, certainly from training once a week with Wycombe. Dave Sexton was a great innovator and believer in aerobic work and developing the capacity to keep going for 90 minutes. We did a lot of cross-country running on Epsom Downs with a set five-and-a-half-mile course which finished on the Epsom Racecourse itself ending with us coming around Tattenham Corner. Every time we did that run I knew how those bloody horses felt. Imagine after you've just done four miles of a sapping run and you're coming around Tattenham Corner as a two-legged human being with that long stretch of incline ahead of you to the finish. It was a punishing, testing ground whether you had four legs or two and often we wondered if we would even make it to the top to meet at the famous pub, the Tattenham Corner.

Fitness was never really an issue at Stamford Bridge, and neither was talent. I was with the group of players in waiting, if you like, behind stars like Ray Wilkins, his brother Graham, Gary Stanley, Steve Finnieston, Tommy Langley, Ian Britton, Ray Lewington and Gary Lock. They were a very talented bunch, in fact we had such a good squad that in season 1973/74 we won the Football Combination, which was the reserve league.

All those players were proteges of Dario Gradi. He brought them into the club, along with chief scout Eddie Heath, and coached them. I soon discovered how good they were and how good the first team was as they trained next to us and that Chelsea senior squad had some exceptional players, like Peter Osgood, and when I saw him up close, as opposed to watching him on television or live, I could see why he was so highly rated. And there were so many players there who were model professionals, pros at the top of their trade. People like Peter Bonetti, John Hollins and Ronnie Harris had reputations which they had earned, Ronnie especially. To most people he was simply a hard man, well he wasn't known as "Chopper" for nothing, but he was a great defender, especially one v one and he was, perhaps, founder member of the "They Shall Not Pass" School of Defending. He excelled when it came to "the ball may get past me, the man may get past me, but not both" fraternity. He was very influential, on and off the pitch, and off it he was extremely quiet.

Chelsea Football Club was a fantastic place to start my career, with so many exceptional players and such a fabulous atmosphere. It certainly impacted on me despite not knowing what the King's Road was, or where it was, but I soon learnt how synonymous the club and that area of London were. It was a showbiz club, always was, and some say it always will be, probably because of its proximity to the West End.

There were always stars from the movies, television and music dropping in. David Soul, also known as Hutch, the blonde one from *Starsky and Hutch*, was a regular visitor as was Richard Attenborough, because he was a big Chelsea fan and he always insisted on being called Dickie. Steve McQueen and Raquel Welch were visitors also, you never knew who was going to turn up next. It didn't matter whether they popped their head around the dressing-room door just before kick-off or mixed with the players in the lounge after the game, the overriding feeling was casual. World-famous stars would mix with celebrity players from the world of football, my world, and it seemed like the most natural thing at a club where celebrity was the norm. It was something I knew nothing of until I joined Chelsea and it happened so often but it was something that quickly enveloped me and something that led to a number of lifelong friendships being established.

It wasn't only lifelong playing friendships that were born at Chelsea. After one game at Stamford Bridge, Lily introduced me to a friend of hers from the Cavern days. She also introduced a girl by the name of Marie Hayward and her husband, Justin, lead singer of the Moody Blues. Marie was a Scouser also and back in the 1960s she had been a girlfriend of George Harrison, around the time Lily was working for the group's fan club. All those people serve to emphasise the close connection between Chelsea FC and show business. We've all remained close friends and meet up whenever possible. In fact it wasn't so long ago when I was attending a Monaco game as part of my role with the Football Association I took Justin Hayward with me as he lives in the south of France. He loves his football despite hailing from Swindon! Some years later when Justin featured on *This is Your Life* Lily and I were invited to the recording of the show and we shared a taxi to the theatre that evening with another guest who turned out to be an astronaut. He was part of Justin's life because apparently he had taken a CD of the Moody Blues' greatest hits with him to the Mir Space Station and was bringing that very CD back to present to Justin in the show.

And show business in 1970s football wasn't restricted to Stamford Bridge. When we used to play at Luton Town Eric Morecambe, the tall one with glasses, who was president of that club, would pop in and see us. There would be a tap on the door and a pair of glasses would appear around the door, shaking up and down.

The downside for me with that show business backdrop was where did football fit in? Chelsea always struck me as being about entertainment, not winning football matches. Let's not forget that the football team had won things. In 1970 it was the FA Cup and the European Cup Winners' Cup the following year, just two years before I arrived but Chelsea were approaching a period, which began in my first season, when the squad began to struggle.

Although my actual debut in the Chelsea first team was home to Newcastle United, as a substitute, my full debut was a couple of weeks later, at Spurs where we won 2-1 with goals from Ron Harris and Mickey Droy. On 13th April 1974 I scored my first goal when we faced Arsenal at home and I was like a fan again because Alan Ball was playing for the Gunners, Alan Ball. I remember thinking: "I'm sharing the same piece of grass as him." I couldn't believe it. We lost 3-1 but I scored, past Bob Wilson. Peter Houseman sent in one of his trademark crosses from the left wing and I took it on my chest and as it dropped, 'woof' it was past Bob in a flash.

I was still in dreamland in my cameo run towards the end of that campaign. Inside two weeks I had made my league debut, my full debut and scored my first goal as a professional footballer but the bubble was about to burst when Dave Sexton left me out of the side. He sat me down and explained he needed a bit more experience in the side as there were a few difficult games coming up and, to be fair, the team was struggling. Indeed for most of that 1973/74 season we were in the lower half of the table and when I got into the side we were still struggling. That win against Tottenham was a rare one so I could see Dave's reasoning and to be fair the experience he put into the side worked and we survived.

The value of experience was brought home to me by an instance in the Arsenal game. Geordie Armstrong made a break down my flank and I chased him something like 60 yards. But he checked, turned me and put in a cross that ended up in the back of our net. Dave asked, in a very aggressive manner, "what was the effing point of chasing him back all that way and, at the death not getting a challenge in". That proved a bit of a lesson for me.

Although we kept ourselves in the First Division a poor start to the following season put Dave Sexton under immense pressure. The team started the campaign with a 2-0 home defeat to newly promoted Carlisle United who won their opening three fixtures to top the First Division table with maximum points. That opening day defeat was followed by another disappointing result at the Bridge, 3-3 against

Burnley, and although the next two games were victories, 3-1 at Coventry and 2-1 at Burnley, the subsequent run of seven games without a win saw us score just three goals and drop to 20th before we beat Tottenham at home 1-0.

If things on the field weren't going well the situation off it simply intensified the pressure Dave was under. He had a few run-ins with senior players who challenged him. Peter Osgood, who he sold to Southampton and Alan Hudson, who joined Stoke, were just a couple of those involved. There was all sorts going on and because most was behind the scenes it made it difficult to understand the politics, the finances of a club that was obviously in trouble and heading down the pan, financially. That led to the departure of players because there obviously wasn't enough money for them. The club wasn't investing in players and that was another sign that all was not well at the Bridge.

Dave had supporters in the dressing room, people like Peter Bonetti, Ron Harris and John Hollins, but there seemed to be a period when players began to leave because the impending financial threat was looming large. It was a period that bridged the time before Dave himself departed and after he had gone. I remember sitting in the stand at Stamford Bridge watching a midweek game, at the time when all the disharmony was bubbling under, and being aware for the first time that such things went on at a football club. It was the unsavoury side of football and I didn't like it. I was an Evertonian and where I came from you supported your club through thick and thin but there I was listening to people all around me, at that game, swearing at Dave, calling him all sorts of names and demanding "get him out". And sitting just in front of me, listening to that barrage of profanity, was Dave's wife.

Not long afterwards Dave was sacked, in October 1974, and replaced by Ron Suart who had been brought to the club by Tommy Docherty as assistant manager and when Dave became manager they retained him. Ron was in charge until April of the following year having been unable to arrest the slide towards inevitable relegation.

Eddie McCreadie, who had been taking the reserves, was placed in caretaker charge for the remainder of that campaign rather than Dario, who had been Dave's assistant. Dario told me he would probably be leaving as well but Dave wasn't unemployed for long and was snapped up by QPR.

I hadn't really figured in the first team towards the end of Dave Sexton's tenure, and was on a one-year contract with a one-year option. Consequently when Dave popped up at Loftus Road Dario told me QPR would be interested in taking me if I was unhappy with my prospects at Chelsea. He didn't think Eddie would want to keep me as I was 23 and there were 18 and 19-year-olds coming through although he had advised Eddie to give me another contract and said that Eddie would speak to me about my situation. That was my 'Damascus' moment. I'd had a go at football as a career, for two years, and it had been fun. I'd achieved something by playing in the top flight and felt I had coped with it so believed I was good enough but the question was whether or not Chelsea agreed.

I was faced with a dilemma. If Eddie offered me a contract did I accept or take up the offer to join Queens Park Rangers, which was very tempting because they had some outstanding players like Stan Bowles and Gerry Francis plus ex-Chelsea players John Hollins and David Webb? Indeed the following season, under Dave Sexton, they finished runners-up to Liverpool in the First Division. But, as a forward, I looked at a squad with internationals like Don Givens and Dave Thomas, and felt I could go there and end up sitting in the stand, watching.

However I looked at it I did have options. Football with Chelsea or QPR or I could follow my previous route into teaching and still play football for a club like Wycombe. So when I sat down with Eddie McCreadie I did have a backup plan. He informed me the club were offering me another contract although it was little more to stay than leave so it was up to me to accept or decline. I reasoned if I couldn't make it at the club at that time, with the players there after the big names had gone, players I had been competing with for two years, then I would be best packing in anyway. I did feel Eddie was intent on making a name for himself by promoting the younger players into the first team slots vacated by the departed stars.

Although we were relegated we had such a talented, hungry group of players that we were able to regain our place in the First Division at the first time of asking, finishing runners-up to Wolves by two points and just ahead of Nottingham Forest, in 1976/77. There was a nucleus of young players; Gary Locke, Ian Britton, Ray and Graham Wilkins, Teddy Maybank, Ray Lewington, Gary Stanley, Steve Wicks and

Steve Finnieston, who played alongside me up front or, I should say, I played alongside him. Although I enjoyed what proved to be my career best season with 13 goals in 36 games in that promotion campaign Steve was the main man with 24 goals in 39 league games, including the winner when we beat Forest 2-1 at home.

Season 1977/78 was to prove a significant period in my life, on and off the field. Originally I was in digs in Raynes Park but as Lily and I grew closer, and I was trekking to and from Liverpool to see her, I decided it was time to get off the fence so I asked her to come down to London and move in with me. We bought a two-bedroom flat in Wimbledon for the princely sum of £16,000 and got married at Morden Registry Office just before Christmas 1977.

It was a Friday, the day before we were to play Fulham and all the gang came down from Liverpool and pitched up at our tiny flat. We held the reception at a pub on Wimbledon Common and it was so unorganised we never even booked a hotel for that night. The flat was so packed there was no room, nor, I have to say, inclination on our part, to spend our first night as a married couple there. We spent hours driving around Richmond Hill and Richmond Park, looking for a bed for the night, eventually finding one in a beautiful hotel at the top of Richmond Hill. Thirty-five years later, and counting, we're still together.

Lily had two sons from her previous marriage, Stephen and Iain, and of course they moved in with us but very soon we outgrew the flat and started looking for a three-bedroom place and it was then I discovered that property development was the game to get into. In 18 months the flat had grown in value to £20,000 so, in percentage terms, it was a fair return on our investment. We moved to a bigger place nearby and I spent a lot of my spare time bashing that about.

By that time Ken Shellito had become Chelsea manager after Eddie McCreadie left. I think Eddie had overstepped the mark a little and the club decided not to offer him a new deal. It was alleged he asked for more than was on offer and that proved an end to negotiations.

I was in the side for a while after Ken took over then I was out of favour and so I had more time for my renovation work back home. It was just ahead of the 1978/79 season when Duncan McKenzie joined Chelsea from Everton. That was great for my wife because Duncan's wife was a friend of Lily and it didn't take long for me to strike up a friendship with Duncan, though he did test that relationship after one episode which was typical for the man who became famous for leaping over Minis and throwing golf balls prodigious distances.

Duncan used to babysit for us and I remember one night we got back home and were greeted, as we entered the living room, by the sight of one wall pitted with marks from little explosions caused by Chinese crackers that had been hurled against it. Hurled against our gorgeous magnolia woodchip wallpaper by our two kids and our 28-year-old babysitter. He thought it was great fun and so did the kids who were safely tucked up in bed.

On the field Duncan was typically flamboyant but the team continued to struggle, winning only once in the opening ten games of 1978/79 so, very early in the campaign, the writing was on the wall again so soon after the previous relegation. I played 15 games and scored four goals but there was an air about the club that didn't augur well for the future, on and off the field, and I couldn't quite put my finger on it. Maybe it was all the showbiz glitz about Chelsea which contradicted the team's lack of impact on the pitch. It was symptomatic of what has proven to be the downfall of many a football person or club.

Football is ego-driven not money-driven. That has always been my view. It's driven by the egos of players. We've all got an ego but some egos are bigger than others. Some egos are controllable, some are unmanageable. Either way you have to have some kind of ego, self-esteem, whatever you call it but there has to be a balance. That was beginning to dominate things at Chelsea, for me. It wasn't so much the coaches and staff but certainly from players and everything surrounding them. That feeling soon morphed into a realisation that I wasn't really achieving anything at the club. As a team we were losing but everyone was happy and losing didn't seem to be affecting people like it should. I looked around at the dominance Liverpool were enjoying and other clubs like Leeds and Arsenal were forging ahead and as I looked around me at Chelsea I was thinking "this can't be right".

All that had happened gradually over a couple of years or so, and of course if you found yourself out of the side and not figuring in the manager's plans it compounded the feeling. It was crazy to find myself back in the reserves especially as I was, by that time, considering myself a professional footballer and this was my livelihood.

It wasn't new to me because it had happened a few times when

Dave Sexton was manager but I was new then and maybe he felt he had to drop me because I was learning and maybe I needed a bit more time to acclimatise and I appreciated his view but it was different under Ken Shellito. I couldn't seem to gain any favour whatever I did. Maybe, crucially, at that time I had been converted from a forward to a midfield player. Ken saw me playing as an attacking midfielder rather than up front. Tommy Langley had also started to bang in the goals and as we approached Christmas it became clear to me that I was surplus to requirements.

Brian Eastick, who had just been appointed youth team coach, told me Aston Villa had been watching me. He knew for sure they had been to a couple of games I played in and Brian told me he knew someone at Villa who confirmed their interest. Then Ken Shellito spoke to me and said that Villa wanted to sign me. Curiously Frank Upton had come to Chelsea, from Villa, to assist Ken and while I got on well with Frank he wasn't really an admirer of me as a footballer.

Football is very insular, like one big family if you like, and there's always a connection. Somebody knows someone else who worked with a close contact who knew someone else so there was a connection linking Frank Upton, with Ron Saunders, at Villa, coming to Chelsea to assist Ken. Neither of them really rated me so making a move to the club from whence Frank had come seemed my best option. Add to that complexity the more simplistic fact that Ken Shellito was very much under pressure due to Chelsea's poor results. Then I got a call saying that Ron Saunders, the Villa manager, wanted to speak to me. I phoned him and he asked me to travel up the next day. He told me to bring my wife with me so we went to Birmingham and on to Bodymoor Heath, the training ground, with Tony Barton, for my first encounter with Ron Saunders.

Goodness me, what a fearsome character Ron was. He was so straight-laced but there was something about him that was so appealing and what he was running at that club. I thought to myself, "this looks like a real football club". It seemed more like what a club should be after what I had been used to over the previous few years and to be fair Duncan McKenzie had embellished it a bit before I set out. Telling me I had to get away from Chelsea and what a fantastic football club Villa was, "The Villa" as he called it. He said it would be a fantastic move for me going to a club with such fabulous heritage and a top club to boot. I don't know if "Duncs" was angling to be my agent but I think the clues were there when he told me: "Make sure you ask for this, that and the other. Make sure you get your holidays paid for, get all your expenses sorted, signing-on fee, make sure it's tax-free." He laid out all these instructions for me and added he would only take 12.5% as his fee! But once I was sat in front of Ron Saunders it didn't seem appropriate. He just sat there with daggers coming out of his eyes and I felt like I was pinned to the wall by his stare. And when we got down to the nitty gritty of money I was looking at just £25 a week more than I was on at Chelsea. But when appearance money and bonuses were added it made the package seem a little better but it wasn't a great deal more than what I was already earning.

Ron told me "take it or leave it". So I went on to the list of 'demands' as outlined by my 'agent' Mr McKenzie who was seated safe and sound 150 miles away, though demands of Ron Saunders doesn't seem the correct word. When I asked, for example, "what about this?" he replied: "Yes, what about it?" Right away that set the tone for the rest of my contract negotiations and I was told that Villa would pay my removal expenses, put me up in a hotel for six months, pay for my travel between London and Birmingham until I got myself sorted but by the start of the next season it was expected I would be living in the area. "There's no ifs, ands or buts. That's the way it is. I'll leave it with you."

I think that was on the Thursday and on the way back to London Lily turned to me and said: "I like him. I think it will be a fantastic move for you." When I queried her assessment, "for £25 a week extra" she pointed out the opportunity that was being presented to me. She added that if I wanted better money I had to go and earn it and she was right. Stars like Andy Gray and Brian Little were part of a very good Villa side. Indeed while I was in London they played in the League Cup Final against Everton and that was only one part of a very successful spell the club was enjoying with another League Cup win as well as finishing second in the league. So there would be no problem about a winning mentality with Aston Villa and I guessed the manager would have no truck with show business or celebrity. So it seemed the right move for me although he was signing me as a striker and, funnily enough, Ron told me he saw me play in the *Daily Express* Five-a-Side Tournament at Wembley, as a striker.

He needed a goalscorer at that time because Andy Gray was out having had surgery on a knee injury. Brian Little was also injured so Ron was going with John Deehan and some other young players like Gordon Cowans, Gary Shaw, Colin Gibson, Gary Williams and Brendan Ormsby. Ironically Chelsea played Villa that very Saturday after my talks with Ron with me out of the Chelsea team watching them play against the club I had a chance of joining. I left Villa Park after telling Ron I would speak to him after the game at Stamford Bridge. I did but only in passing and told him I would be coming. However, the next day, I had a call from Chelsea chairman Brian Mears. He told me they were going to change the manager and my move to Villa was off because I might be staying. I didn't know what to think but I knew I would have to wait, at least until Monday, to see what transpired. I think Ken Shellito went that weekend so the whole situation was in the melting pot.

So come Monday morning Chelsea had a new manager in place, Frank Upton. He phoned me to tell me what I already knew, that Ken had gone and he was in charge. Then he said: "The first decision I am making is, you can go." No beating about the bush and it did seem he was trying to make an impact with his first decision as manager. No matter, for me it was my get out of jail card so off I went to Birmingham to sign as a Villa player.

Tony Barton met me and took me to Ron Saunders' house in Solihull where we met Ron's wife, Breda, and sat down to a cup of tea with Villa's vice-chairman Harry Kartz, who had come along to welcome me to the club. That really made me feel special and I remember photographs being taken and thinking "I bet he's got photographs with all the players Villa have signed". The fee agreed was £100,000, or so I was told, and while, on paper, that looked to be a significant amount, Trevor Francis became the first million-pound transfer in that same season. There was no kudos in being a £100,000 player. In fact, truth be told, I felt Villa had got a "snip", for a 26-year-old player, if Trevor was a million.

After signing on the dotted line I couldn't wait to get started and went in for my first day's training the next morning.

Chapter 4

The Villa

I quickly realised I had made the best decision of my life joining Villa. It began as early as day one, when I reported for training. It was so different to that which had been the norm for me. It was more professional, more organised and the training was serious. There was a competitive edge to everything we did at Bodymoor, Ron Saunders saw to that. I could see they were pros and it was easy to see why they had been successful and why what I was leaving behind wasn't. I'm not having a go at the Chelsea players, it was more the regime that allowed that situation to prevail. A situation where there was little substance but at Villa I found the complete opposite.

What a setting Villa Park presented on match day, the culmination of all that professional training. You were a goal up before kick-off thanks to that crowd. There was a buzz about the place, an expectation that you won at home, different to how it had been at Chelsea. If Ron Saunders had a presence, Aston Villa Football Club had it in abundance.

I didn't have to wait long for my debut, Saturday 16th December at home to Norwich City, wearing the number nine shirt and we drew 1-1. Our goal was actually a Mick Maguire own goal and it was Mick who gave me a coaching job, via the PFA, when I retired from playing.

I also broke a finger in that game. But the crowd reinforced my feeling that I had joined a proper football club after seemingly going nowhere for the last couple of years at Chelsea. After Norwich we drew five consecutive games, the fifth a 1-1 draw at Old Trafford in which I scored my first Villa goal.

I remember we hit United on the counter-attack and as I slipped the ball past Gary Bailey, Arthur Albiston lunged desperately to try and stop the ball going in but only succeeded in getting tangled up with it in the back of the net. I remember thinking "s**t, I hope he doesn't try to claim it". That goal is recorded in some archives as an Arthur Albiston own goal but I never got that many goals so in my book it was my first for Aston Villa.

I had to wait until my seventh game before I scored my first goal at Villa Park, on 7th March in a 3-0 victory over Bolton. On 28th April Villa entertained Chelsea and I remember that game vividly because it was such a big, nervous occasion for me being the first time I faced them since I left. I was anxious because of the nature of my last couple of years at Stamford Bridge where I had really been stewing. After six months at Villa and going as well as my new team was I thought I had proved my point. Chelsea were slipping down the league by then and their defeat that day certainly didn't help their cause. Tommy Langley put Chelsea ahead but Graham Wilkins put through his own goal for our equaliser then, right on script, I scored the winner past "The Cat" Peter Bonetti.

Although the question of goals became less pertinent as my career progressed, after I was converted to a defender, it was never the less a good first campaign for Villa in terms of goals. After that winner against Chelsea I scored in the next game against a team that was flying at that time, Ipswich under Bobby Robson.

I was an ever-present for the rest of that debut season and even managed five goals. It's interesting to look back to that period when consistency was a feature as it was to be a critical factor when Aston Villa won the First Division title in 1981 but from a personal perspective I was delighted to take my unbroken run of appearances to 53 before getting injured against Brighton in 1979/80.

Villa finished eighth in my first season and that further underlined what a good move it was for me. I remember thinking "this is more like it, this is what I want". I wanted to be pushing towards the top of the First Division, I wanted to win things and be successful. The realisation of that ambition wasn't too far away although when I went to Aston Villa as a forward I never imagined that I would win trophies as a defender.

I think 1979/80 proved to be a turning point in my career because it was during that campaign I finally converted from being a forward. I was never really a striker in the accepted sense and never saw myself as a great goal threat. I usually played most effectively just off a front man, as I had with Steve Finnieston at Chelsea, or wide on the flank of a four-man midfield. but all that changed in October 1979.

We drew 0-0 at home to West Brom and were due to play Derby County the following Saturday. Ron told me, before selecting me at full-back at the Baseball Ground, that we would talk on the coach afterwards. We won 3-1 and on the way back he sat next to me and asked "well, how did it go then?" I thought I'd done okay, which seemed to please him because he said: "Good, because I think you can do this. I think you can play there but have a think about it because I'm going to play you at right-back for the next few weeks and we'll see how it goes."

That was to prove a catalyst because he told me the top and bottom of the situation was, if I was comfortable enough at right-back he would buy a forward. If I wasn't then he said he would sign a right-back, to replace John Gidman. But Ron added if I chose to remain a forward I would, as he put it, "be in the swim with all the other forwards", and we had some decent forwards then including David Geddis, John Deehan, Brian Little and Gary Shaw so it wasn't much of a decision for me. It was also a massive vote of confidence and when I look back on my career I enjoyed my time as a full-back which I actually found quite easy.

As well as my switch of position October 1979 was also significant for another reason. It was the month in which I scored my last goal for Aston Villa and it was another of the ironies that seem to punctuate my career because that goal came against Everton in the third round of the League Cup. We were held 0-0 at Villa Park so had to replay at Goodison Park. The fact I scored on the ground where I worshipped as a kid was no consolation as we were stuffed 4-1.

Curiously it wasn't the absolute end of my career as a forward and later that season, because of a striker crisis at the club, Ron had to ring the changes. Gary Shaw and Brian Little were injured, Brian with the knee injury that would eventually end his career. John Deehan had already left for West Brom so Ron was forced to implement a makeshift strike-force comprising myself and Allan Evans. We played together up front for three consecutive games, hardly setting the place on fire. In fact neither of us scored in that run although Allan did score against Nottingham Forest in the game that saw me revert to right-back, which perhaps tells its own story.

What was very pleasing for me and the rest of the lads that season was the progress we were making and finishing seventh was an improvement on the previous campaign. It was obviously a transitional period for Villa and slowly but surely Ron was assembling a young and talented squad but perhaps his most significant signing was Peter Withe, who was nearly 30 by the time he became the club's record signing at £500,000, in May 1980. Peter had made his name at Nottingham Forest where he had won the league championship, the League Cup and the Charity Shield.

I think it's also significant that a handful of players played in nearly all the games that season, forming the foundation for what was going to be a record season ahead for Aston Villa. It's incredible that Ron Saunders used just 14 players in winning the First Division title in 1980/81. It's even more astonishing that seven of us played in every single game: Jimmy Rimmer, Des Bremner, Gordon Cowans, Dennis Mortimer, Ken McNaught, Tony Morley and myself. Allan Evans and Gary Shaw missed just three league games and Peter Withe played 40 out of the 46 matches in all competitions. Two years earlier, when Liverpool won the title, they used one player more than we did. I think everyone in football knows that in those days it was commonplace to play with an injury. I could count on the fingers of one hand when I felt 100% fit going into a game. We all played carrying a knock of some sort, it wasn't macho you just wanted to play. Of course it wouldn't happen nowadays because there is greater awareness of the potential for damage when playing not fully fit than there was 30 years ago. But then, as now, the players' say-so was often the final arbiter.

I really admired Kenny Dalglish, one of the best players I ever faced. I used to look at the goals he got and the number of games he played in his position leading the attack for all those years. You can't tell me he was 100% fit because he must have taken some right whacks and kickings. That was why I admired him so much. Indeed I always respected players who had not only a special talent but who turned out for their team, week in week out, whatever injury they might have been carrying, real team players with team spirit. That's what we had at Aston Villa and it helped bring a first league title to the club for 71 years.

We made a good start to 1980/81, winning three and drawing one of the opening four fixtures but then we lost to the team who would go neck-and-neck with us for the league championship, Ipswich Town. Frans Thijssen, who I would later play with at Nottingham Forest, scored the only goal at Portman Road. We lost the next game, to Everton, of course, but then commenced the first of two long unbeaten runs which proved the backbone of our success.

We recovered to beat Wolves and the only blemish in a winning sequence of nine was a thrilling 3-3 draw at Old Trafford. So things on the pitch could not have been better but off it we were getting merciless stick from the media for the incentive scheme and bonuses we were on. Because we were winning so often it meant, with midweek games, we could more than double our wages. Unfortunately, somehow the press got hold of the idea that we were earning extortionate amounts of money. But it must be remembered there were some top players, on £1,000 a week and more, at that time and for us to be in that kind of company we had to be sitting on top of the league and we were.

To be fair to Ron he did defend us, like any good manager should. We were professional footballers at the top of our profession and the club's attitude, quite rightly, was we can afford it. From the players' perspective it was not an issue at all. It may have become an issue further down the line but I can state categorically that the incentives and bonuses were not a factor in us winning the league that year. The money never came into it yet some people would say "you'd kick your granny for that kind of money". It just wasn't true, not in my experience, certainly not in the teams I played in and not for the vast majority of footballers I played with. Money was not the motivator, it was the satisfaction of victory and the esteem that brought.

We had few hiccups that season and in the main we were in the groove and stayed there. Peter Withe was scoring goals, so was Gary Shaw and, very importantly, we were getting goals from elsewhere. Tony Morley scored ten league goals, Allan Evans got seven and "Sid"

Cowans weighed in with five. We were also solid at the back and only conceded more than two goals in a game twice, ironically in the league games against Manchester United which both ended 3-3.

We weren't appreciated in all quarters, it has to be said. I think there was always a feeling that Ipswich were regarded as easier on the eye than us because they had some fantastic players. I wouldn't disagree with that. There was Frans Thijssen, Arnold Muhren, Mick Mills, Eric Gates, George Burley, John Wark and Paul Mariner and a fantastic manager in Bobby Robson, who was obviously in the ascendancy then. Indeed it was a mark of just how good they were that they beat us three times that season, twice in the league and also in the FA Cup, 1-0, and we only managed one goal against them in all those games.

For most of that campaign it seemed a two-horse race between us and Ipswich but Arsenal weren't far behind. Liverpool were a little off the pace but compensated by winning the European Cup and my mate Terry McDermott was even outscoring Kenny Dalglish. It was certainly a more open top flight than it is now. These days the talk is about the top four or five as an almost exclusive club but back then there were more teams who could challenge towards the top. And if you did finish top you reaped the reward of playing in the European Cup whereas these days you can qualify for the Champions League by finishing fourth. Back then if you finished fourth you played in the Uefa Cup.

As Villa and Ipswich entered the spring of 1981, we were keeping up the pressure on each other at the top of the table. In the games before our fixture in mid-April, as Ipswich were winning six in a row we were winning seven. Going down to Highbury for the final game of the season, with so much riding on it, for the first time I think we felt pressure although that began around the time of that game against Ipswich, on 14th April.

Nearly 48,000 fans packed in for what was an evening game at Villa Park and for most footballers games played under floodlights are a little bit more special. It's as if the floodlights are simply huge spotlights that highlight the game below and you get such a wonderful atmosphere. I always preferred playing in the evening because I always felt at my best then as opposed to a Saturday afternoon. You could have a good kip for a day game and it can be a good sleep or a bad one but once you have had it, that's it, you kicked off at three but if you had a bad kip the night before a night game you could have a hour or two to make up for it before the evening kick-off. There also tended to be a bit of dew on the grass for the later starts and that added to the whole setting.

So the scene was set for the crucial game with Ipswich. We were a goal down at half-time and never got back into it so for the third time that season they had done us and despite the fact we were still top of the table it did seem the writing was on the wall. But after that defeat something quite extraordinary happened.

From the gloom that was almost tangible in our dressing room we could hear the noise and euphoria coming from the Ipswich dressing room. The walls were reverberating with their celebrations and it seemed they regarded the title race as over. They were celebrating so much and because it was so quiet where we were it simply magnified everything, their joy and our despair. But as all that evolved over the 20 minutes or so it took us to get showered and changed and the hype surrounding the game and the spring the Ipswich players had in their step as they were leaving, something happened.

It was quite surreal. The Villa players started to look around at each other and, as one, the thought spread among us, "they think it's all over". No one actually said it but we were thinking it and rather than licking our wounds, the next day we were licking our lips. It was such a motivating factor for us to witness the Ipswich response. It was a feeling I only ever experienced once more in my career, when I was at Forest.

We got back on track by beating Forest 2-0, and drawing with Stoke before winning 3-0 at home to Middlesbrough while Ipswich shot themselves in the foot by losing two in a row. That threw up a situation on the final Saturday which looked set to decide the title. Villa went to Arsenal needing to get a better result than Ipswich who were at Middlesbrough.

There was a massive crowd at Highbury which underlined what a tall order it was to try and get something out of Arsenal. In fact I struggle to recall ever getting anything from there during my entire career, if I got over the halfway line I had done well. They were a top side and whenever I faced them my toughest ever opposition was a combination of Graham Rix and Kenny Sansom. They both had pace and ability and in Kenny you had a great defender while Graham was a talented footballer who could whip crosses in from any angle and any distance. You might think you had him trapped and in a flash he was gone and the ball was flighted in behind you. As a partnership they were the best I ever had to cope with. They could defend, they could attack, and were very strong and a very good part of a very good team.

I remember thinking as we went into that game we would do well to get a draw, something we were capable of. I think the general scenario was that we would be okay with a draw but if we lost we would end up praying. Fifteen minutes in we were 1-0 down to a Willie Young goal so we had to chase the game but managed to force a corner just before half-time, at the North Bank end. Dennis Mortimer took the kick which was cleared upfield. The ball was hoisted high in the air and this young lad, Brian McDermott, gave chase. He was quick and so was I but he was about nine years younger and as the ball bounced over my head he was on it in a flash and haring away towards goal, with me trailing in his wake. He took one touch and Jimmy Rimmer raced off his line while I'm trying desperately to hang on in Brian's slipstream. I remember a last-ditch attempt by me, and thinking "b******s" as he closed in on the edge of the box. I swung a leg at him and to hell with the consequences because in those days it wasn't an automatic sending-off. I caught Brian but not as well as I intended and he stumbled a little but still managed to get a toe on the ball which forced it past Jimmy and I can still see, to this day, how it rolled agonisingly towards the goal. I think it only just managed to cross the line but as soon as it did the whole ground erupted.

As I lay on the ground, Brian having well and truly done me, I'm thinking "s**t, 2-0". I had run half the length of the pitch hacking away at this young kid and failed miserably. I was praying the ground would open up and bury me, along with our title aspirations. Two goals to nil, away to Arsenal, forget it. For the first time in my life, and many people would have had the experience, I felt the sands of time, or at least the Football League championship, slipping through my fingers, having had such a joyride with Chelsea and joining Villa and chasing the title. Not bad for a Kirkby kid but that was later, at a little shy of 4.45pm on 2nd May 1981. After Arsenal's second goal I lay there feeling I had cost Aston Villa the league. I took the whole thing personally. I went in at half-time and it was deathly silent as we sat in the changing room trying to be upbeat. Ron was calm in stating that Arsenal got "two goals out of nothing so just keep doing all the good things you've been doing all season". It was all positive stuff and I remember it easing my mind a little and that helped as we went out for the second half, but the truth of it was Aston Villa didn't play very well that day.

But with about 15 minutes to go, and us still chasing the game, I think we were attacking the Clock End and the ball went out of play on my side, in the Arsenal half. I went to retrieve the ball and because it had gone into the crowd I moved towards a section of supporters and all of a sudden there was a huge roar which reverberated around Highbury. The Arsenal supporters where I went for the ball were all thumbs up towards me shouting "yehhhh" and laughing at me and the whole of the Clock End, where our supporters were gathered, was bouncing up and down. The home supporters near me were shouting "Boro are 2-1 up, Ipswich are losing". I took the throw and quickly looked around at my team-mates and although we couldn't talk because we were too busy with the game there was a definite positive vibe about their body language so it was safe to assume something to our benefit was happening at Ayresome Park. Sure enough two Bosko Jankovic goals saw Boro fight back from 1-0 down at half-time to win 2-1 and hand us the title. Some years later I bumped into Bosko and shook his hand, bought him a drink and thanked him, saying I would never forget the day he got those goals and telling him he would never know what they meant to Aston Villa.

We struggled to get off the Highbury pitch that day because the fans swarmed on at the final whistle but the news soon filtered through that Ipswich had lost to Middlesbrough and Villa were league champions for the first time since 1910. But I have to say it was a bitter sweet moment because things had been so desperate at half-time. Having got through it I felt something, fate perhaps, decided there should be justice at the end. You don't win leagues with one result and it then dawned on me. Just because you've lost one game, it doesn't mean anything. It wasn't a cup final that day, it was the last of 42 cup finals we had played and we'd won most of those cup finals, 26 to be precise, so we were worthy champions. Any team that wins the league are worthy champions because at the end of the season the table is what it is. Anyone who watches football, plays football or works in football knows the stats don't lie.

The champagne flowed in the dressing room afterwards, and

beyond. We celebrated all the way back to Birmingham and a week later we did the mandatory open-top bus tour of the city and what makes that time even more pleasurable and proud for me concerns my youngest son, Tom, who wasn't even a twinkle in the eye then. These days he works for a firm of lawyers based in Victoria Square, in Birmingham, overlooking the balcony from which we brandished the league championship trophy at the conclusion of our procession that day so when he looks out of his office window, while engaged in his day to day job, he can see where his two brothers stood with me and the trophy.

We can all look back on that historic season – players, supporters and pundits – and seek to analyse what made Aston Villa, a team that finished eighth and seventh in the seasons prior to 1980/81, champions. There wasn't one single factor, more a combination, all sorts of things contributed to success. On reflection any neutral watching Villa then would have said we were a very physically fit running side as opposed to Ipswich who really had some graceful players and, to use that phrase again, were easier on the eye. But in terms of efficiency and doggedness we had those attributes in abundance. We were hard to beat and when we got in front it was tough to pull back that advantage. When we were a goal down it never used to faze us and more often than not we could get back into a match. I think our fitness regime contributed to all those facets of our game, for a couple of years at least. We also had some terrific players and although we only used 14 players most of them could pop up with a goal or several. Even Dave Geddis, who only played eight times in the league, got the perfect striker ratio of a goal every other game. And of course we had the ideal strike partnership of Gary Shaw and Peter Withe. Gary got 18 in 40 league matches and Peter finished with a more than impressive 20 in 36.

Although I had been promoted with Chelsea, winning the league championship with Villa gave me my first winner's medal. But I also picked up the first of two consecutive awards that figure just as highly in my personal collection – being voted into the PFA First Division team. When you consider at that time that Phil Neal and Viv Anderson were the top two right-backs in the top division, and England internationals to boot, it puts me making the PFA team, voted for by the pros, our peers, into some kind of perspective, for me anyway.

I have, on occasion, been asked why I never played for England.

The answer is I came close, very close, but it never happened. It was the end of that Villa title-winning campaign and I was sat at home on the Sunday enjoying a glass of wine with our dinner and I got a phone call from Ron Saunders. Sobering up quickly to ensure I could string a sentence together I picked up the phone and after exchanging the usual pleasantries he said: "Do you fancy joining the England squad?" I said: "Pardon?" He added: "Do you fancy joining the England squad? They're playing Brazil next week and then they have the Home Internationals afterwards. Ron Greenwood has just called me and he's without Phil Neal because of the European Cup Final and Viv Anderson is injured so he wanted to know if you were available and my opinion about you so do you fancy going down?"

I thought "wow" and pulled myself together and asked for details of where and when. I found it difficult to take in as I came off the phone. I was tingling and could feel it up and down my body. As if winning the league wasn't enough, to be given the chance of an England cap was out of this world, out of my world anyway, especially considering my age. I had never thought I would get the chance even though I had made the PFA First Division team. It was a foretaste of the irony that surrounded my move to Nottingham Forest, also due to a Viv Anderson injury. I set off for Enfield the next morning and was so excited in my eagerness to get there I was oblivious to the speed I was doing and picked up my first speeding ticket.

Coming out of Birmingham on the A45 I was stopped by the police, for doing something like 47 mph in a 30 zone. When the patrol car pulled me over it was almost like a comedy sketch on TV. The officer, who I hoped was a Villa fan, came over and tapped on my window, which I wound down. "Hello sir, we in a hurry are we? Where are you heading?" I told him who I was and where I was going, adding: "You have to forgive me because I'm going down to meet up with the England squad." I should have guessed his mood from his succinct reply, "must I now. Who do you play for?" "Aston Villa," I mumbled.

"Not your lucky day Ken, is it?" he said as he slapped the ticket into my hand. I thought he was going to say, "that's terrific, off you go now and take care". It was another 20 years before I picked up my second ticket.

Driving a bit more conservatively I eventually made the England camp at West Lodge Park and I have to say that my initial impressions were less than favourable. It all seemed a bit loose. I got there early, two hours before anyone else. Brazil was a midweek fixture and although I never made the bench I was in the squad and got the chance to don my England garb in which to watch the game. After the match we went back home for a couple of days before reporting back for the Home Internationals.

To be fair to Ron Greenwood he did say he hoped I would enjoy the experience and promised by the end of the trip I would have a cap. He wasn't specific as to which game but the promise was there which made me feel ten feet tall. I thought to myself, "all I have to do is live, wake up for the next week or so and I'll end up with an England cap".

When the players began reporting to the hotel they did so in dribs and drabs but what struck me was the topic of conversation which, even back then, was money. Players' pool money, how much was in the kitty for the World Cup etc. Kevin Keegan's agent was handling that side of things but that was just symptomatic of how lax things seemed, to the Aston Villa players at least, who were used to a tighter ship under Ron Saunders. I thought the players at England seemed to hold a bit more sway, it certainly didn't feel like a football club. It was a strange atmosphere, strange culture.

Once all the players were assembled the next topic of conversation was where they were going that night. Some were going over to Bob Wilson's house, which wasn't far away, though most targeted a local pub, The White Hart in Southgate, a regular watering hole for the England squad then. Being new to the set-up we, Dennis Mortimer, Peter Withe and myself, didn't want to seem oddballs and wish everyone a good night before shooting off to bed so we decided to tag along.

We spent a few hours chatting and having a few pints and as closing time loomed Peter Withe, who I had gone with, alongside Dennis Mortimer and Viv Anderson, the driver, said it was time to go. Some of the England regulars, the more senior players, said that there was no need to go because when the pub was cleared we could stay on and have a drink afterwards, a lock-in basically. Again, not wishing to be shrinking violets we decided to stay. Next thing I knew it was past midnight and despite the game not being until the Wednesday I thought it best to go back so our group departed, leaving most of the squad behind.

As we pulled into the hotel forecourt Viv exited the car first and went over towards the entrance and looked into one of the windows and I'll never forget what happened next.

Viv had the biggest smile in the world and the most expressive face. He turned back towards the rest of us and voiced rather than verbalised, as he pointed. "The gaffer, the f*****g gaffer's in there." We chuckled, quietly, and went along with him. "Yeh, of course he is, nice one Viv." We casually entered the foyer, hands in pockets with not a care in the world until we turned our heads to note, sitting next to the large open fire were; coach Bill Taylor, the doctor, Don Howe and Ron Greenwood, just as the clock was chiming 12.30am. And there's us, grown-ups, but nervously wondering what to say, or not.

Viv, as a slightly older hand than us England virgins, spoke, saying: "We've only been down to the local and had a few drinks." "That's all we need," was all Ron said, because there had been some recent bad publicity involving some England players at a nightclub abroad. But after a few "goodnights" were exchanged we sloped off to bed and left them to their fireside chat which no doubt would centre on us. The next morning as I was leaving my room I bumped into Tony Woodcock. I asked him what time he'd come in the night before, remembering that he was teetotal. He said it was after one but before 2am. Then I asked him "what did they say?" "Who?" he replied. "There was no one here so we all just went to our rooms."

The rest of our preparation passed uneventfully and I was named as one of the substitutes for the game against Wales on the Wednesday night. Kenny Sansom was playing left-back and he got injured in the second half and for the first time in my life, in my head anyway, I'm screaming "stay down" because I was desperate to get on. Hoping it was "terminal", I just waited for the sight of Kenny limping off and me getting the nod. But like the Trojan he was Kenny got to his feet and that was my chance gone. I guess I might have got the promised cap in the next game, against Northern Ireland in Belfast, but that never happened either. Because of civil unrest the Home Office decided that it was too risky to play there and neither England nor Wales were prepared to fulfil the fixture so, for me, that only left the final Home International against Scotland and I wasn't involved.

In looking back at Villa's title-winning season something else stands out for me, but whether or not it was a factor I don't know. I know Gary Shaw was the only local lad in our team but there was a Scouse nucleus. Dennis Mortimer and myself were from Kirkby and proud of it. Peter Withe was from Liverpool. Tony Morley was from Ormskirk and Jimmy Rimmer was from the posh part, Southport, so half the team had been brought up in an area steeped in football culture and that was a feature of football then, especially in big cities like Liverpool, Manchester and Newcastle. I'm not sure that's the case these days.

Many point to the consistency brought about by so many players from only 14 used being ever-present. But many also point out to the re-energised Tony Morley who at times that season was unplayable and that was down to Ron Saunders.

Tony was a great character, a very confident player who certainly brought panache to the football field. He was two-footed, could cross a ball with either foot, had lovely close ball control and could score goals. There were other players like that then but Tony was more of a goal threat and being two-footed he could play comfortably on either flank so was a terrific asset, but it was Ron Saunders who turned him into the player he became for us.

There was an amazing working relationship between Tony and Ron because he feared Ron and knew he had to please him otherwise the manager would drag him off the field, put the sub on and leave him out the following week. Ron had that stick all the time. It was always a carrot and stick with Tony and more stick than anything else. There always seemed to be a running battle between them as far as Ron's demands were concerned but there is no doubt that Tony was a big crowd favourite. Ron knew that and knew how far he could push Tony but basically, he was a wonderful player.

I remember we didn't have the best of starts to the following season, in fact we had a shocking result to kick off the campaign when we lost 1-0 at home to newly promoted Notts County. If consistency was the mark of the title-winning season it was the complete opposite in 1981/82 as far as our league form was concerned and it was to be a recurring theme during that season which was to finish with us as European champions.

We only won one of our opening nine games and had six consecutive draws until we won against West Ham and Wolves. It was really disappointing, indeed staggering for us to fall away like that, and the drop off was reflected in lower average attendances. We were conscious that we were poor but it was different when it came to the European Cup.

I can't explain why other than to highlight the expectation surrounding the quest for European success and as the domestic season wore on and we became less and less capable of clawing our way back into the top three or four the European Cup became more central to our focus and as we progressed through the rounds the expectation grew. That was to be expected around the club but it spread nationwide and grew in intensity as a consequence.

The expectation of the entire country was understandable as English clubs had won the European Cup in the five years before we set out and the pressure on Villa to complete six in a row was enormous. But, in many respects, I think it stood us in good stead because we didn't play as well as we could have done in some of those European ties, but I always felt, whenever we stepped out against any European opposition in that season, we were a goal up before a ball was kicked. That was simply down to the awe in which English clubs were held abroad because of the consistency of this country when it came to winning the trophy, so why wouldn't it happen again? There was also an element of "where did they come from" which had been applied to Nottingham Forest before they won it twice and I think Villa were bracketed in that same category. So I felt that winning pedigree gave us a distinct advantage.

It was also noticeable when we ran out against continental teams, sometimes their body language would say a lot about their mindset, facing an English side. It wasn't quite rabbit in the headlights but you could see by their demeanour that they felt they were going to have their work cut out that night. And let's be fair, we did play a different type of game to the European teams. I think it's more uniform now around Europe but I do feel we are still unique. Okay so that assertion was a little exposed in the Champions League Final of 2011 but Barcelona have been the best for a number of years and the rest of Europe are not like Barca. There was certainly no team around like Barcelona when we entered the European Cup but it was almost like we had two separate seasons in the one in terms of the disparity between our progress in Europe and lack of it back home. Throw into the mix the situation behind the scenes at the club and it makes our win in Rotterdam even more commendable.

There are always internal politics, at most clubs anyway. Thankfully such wranglings are usually kept well away from the playing side but can occasionally spill over. One such occurrence came midway through the season which left us fourth from the bottom of the table, with a caretaker manager, and a European Cup quarter-final against Dynamo Kiev around the corner. It was certainly a long way, in every respect, from Aston Villa's first ever game in Europe's premier club competition, in September, against Valur Reykjavik.

The first game turned out to be fairly easy and we won 5-0 at home leaving the proverbial formality in Iceland. It may have only been September but it was cold, I remember that. I don't remember too much about the game which we won 2-0, but THE abiding memory was the location of the Valur ground, right next to a fish factory. The air was heavy with the stench of fish so we were more than happy to make a successful and speedy getaway and so the adventure began.

Round two was an altogether different prospect, Dynamo Berlin. I never played in the away game but we got a terrific result in the first leg in Germany by winning 2-1 with a couple of Tony Morley goals. But we almost slipped up at Villa Park and went down 1-0 but squeezed through on away goals. That was the fright of the tournament for us and although I don't remember too much about the tie I do remember us hanging on for dear life at Villa Park. I also recall after the game thinking we had been given an early taste of what life was like at the top table of European football. We'd had a doddle of a game in the first round and nearly been knocked out in the second and there was still a long way to go. Welcome to the European Cup boys.

Then things started getting really serious because we were through to face Dynamo Kiev in the quarter-final. I remember that tie more than anything and of course, beforehand, we had the situation behind the scenes which resulted in Ron Saunders and Villa parting company.

We were all shell-shocked when Ron resigned and I think it was the day before a midweek game against Southampton, at Villa Park, which made it an even bigger shock. The story we heard was that Ron had been seeking a rollover contract so that he, in the event of being sacked, would get a decent severance deal. I believe that Ron Bendall, the majority shareholder at the time, turned Ron's request down and without hesitation he resigned. It was quite unbelievable. Not the actual event because that kind of thing happens all the time in football but it was the timing that blew us away. From a personal perspective I wondered where that would leave me because it was Ron who brought me to Villa, nurtured me and turned me into the player I had become. He was the one who had my absolute respect.

In those days the players used to drop into our usual watering hole for a drink after a game before going home but on that particular day after Ron resigned, there was a very sombre air about our gathering as we sought some kind of sense from a situation that had none. Knowing that Ron liked a glass of brandy I bought a bottle for him which I was going to drop in on the way home. I remember stopping the taxi at his house in Solihull and going up his drive and leaving the bottle, with a card, next to his empty milk bottles, thanking him for everything he did for me. Ron wasn't in at the time but came in to the club the next day to say his goodbyes and it was a very emotional occasion.

Ironically I understand Ron did get the very contract he wanted, inside nine days of his resignation, just down the road when he turned up as manager of Birmingham City, which didn't go down well with die-hard Villa fans. In doing so he became the first former Aston Villa manager to take charge of the Blues.

Tony Barton took the reins at Villa and everyone knew Tony and he knew the place inside out and though he was short of managerial and coaching experience he did really well, even being named Manager of the Month for April 1982. He managed the situation very well having risen from chief scout, and being integral to my signing for Villa, through assistant manager to finally sitting in the boss's seat itself. When his appointment as permanent manager was eventually confirmed on 1st April, the irony was not lost on anyone, least of all Tony.

And to be fair to Tony it would have been easy for him to tinker with things because we hadn't played well, in the league, all season. To his credit he left a well-oiled machine to run itself. Everything was in place and going into games little motivation was required, though some of the fans may not have agreed with that particular sentiment, but to some extent not tinkering with something is as much a skill as tinkering.

We flew out to take on Kiev, with Tony having been in charge for three weeks, to face a team that were winners of the European Cup Winners' Cup and Super Cup a few years earlier, a much tougher prospect than the Dynamo team beaten by Villa the previous round.

That tie was memorable for the journey we had in getting over for the first leg because the first game was postponed and moved to Simferopol, in the Crimea, where the Yalta meeting between Churchill, Roosevelt and Stalin had taken place. It proved an ordeal with two long flights and stopovers and there was always an air of cloak and dagger in those days when you travelled beyond the Iron Curtain. Then there was the food, fish eye soup, which was dreadful and when we got there the beds were awful. They were only about five feet long so I don't know if most Ukrainians were short or what but I do remember Ken McNaught, Peter Withe and the two goalkeepers with their calves hanging over the end of the bed and there were no toilets, but thankfully there were a few sinks!

The conditions in the hotel were spartan to say the least so we were glad to get the game under way which brought us face to face with the other memorable feature of that tie, Oleg Blokhin, one of the top players in the world and 1975 European Footballer of the Year. He was an awesome figure and a very powerful striker with power and pace and a superb left foot. He was one of the few players in those days who could win a game on his own. So we did really well keeping him in check in the away game, particularly the centre-halves, to get a 0-0 result. Then after the match we attended a social function at which we had the mandatory smashing of vodka glasses in the fireplace.

We finished the job at Villa Park with Gary Shaw and Ken McNaught getting our goals to set up a semi-final tie with Anderlecht, who were the most successful Belgian club in Europe having won the Cup Winners' Cup twice. Indeed they played in three consecutive finals in the 1970s, as well as twice picking up the Super Cup, so they were going to be formidable opponents and more proof that the further you went in the European Cup the better your opposition became.

Tony Morley scored the only goal in the Villa Park first leg so although we only took a slender lead to Brussels we viewed it from the positive perspective that Anderlecht had missed their chance of getting an away goal. I think if you manage an away goal in the first leg then you have something in the bank and if you don't then the opposition get their chance. And our result at home was our fourth successive clean sheet in Europe. In fact after that first semi-final game we won three league games in a row and kept a clean sheet each time so we went into the second leg full of confidence having not conceded a goal in four games.

Of course Anderlecht put us under immense pressure but we kept our heads and more importantly kept the ball and maintained our concentration, which is so crucial at the top level, especially against European teams. Unfortunately events off the field overtook events on it and there was fighting among rival supporters and some fans invaded the pitch and the game was held up. It interrupted the flow of the game which seemed to affect Anderlecht more than us. I didn't think it was that big an issue but after we got through with a 0-0 draw Anderlecht tried to have the game replayed and then lobbied Uefa to have Villa expelled from the competition, but they were unsuccessful.

At the end of the month Uefa did take action and fined Villa £14,500 and Anderlecht were also penalised to the tune of around £4,000 but the most important outcome was us being cleared to play the final against Bayern Munich.

We had more than a month before we played the final so attention switched back to our domestic programme which had really suffered due to our European focus. And the phrase has to be "switched back" because we were distracted. Not before Christmas but after the Berlin game as the European Cup grew in importance because of course we had the break from November until the competition resumed in March, the quarter-final stage, so we knew we had that to look forward to. We did go some way to recovering our league form and in the February we had a decent run but on reflection we knew, as a group, during that period over the end of the year and into 1982 that we were never really going to make any impact on the top group of the First Division so the European Cup was our only realistic opportunity of success.

We were totally relaxed in the build-up to the European Cup Final. We were underdogs managed by someone who was so anonymous, outside England, that the Aston Villa coach in the programme for the final was listed as Jim Paul, our kit man! Jim, who sadly died a few years back, certainly appreciated his moment in the spotlight.

A couple of years ago I met a Villa fan who told me he couldn't make it to Rotterdam so had to watch on television. He told me the body language of the Villa players was so relaxed as they wandered around the Feyenoord Stadium, taking photographs. And that's exactly how it was and there was one very good explanation for that. We were in uncharted territory and for that reason alone we were unafraid because, never having experienced that before, we didn't know what to be afraid of so we could tell ourselves we could just enjoy the occasion, we might not come again. Having said that, I didn't feel like that but equally I didn't feel too nervous about it. I had become more and more confident in our ability to keep going as we progressed through the rounds as the teams we faced became harder and harder to beat. So I went into the final not thinking for a moment that we would lose, even though they had Rummenigge, Breitner, Augenthaler, Hoeness etc etc, some bloody good players.

Three decades on most Villa fans only remember three things about the 1982 European Cup Final, apart from winning of course. It was a very poor game, Peter Withe scored a scrappy winner and the injury to Jimmy Rimmer in the early minutes of the contest.

I knew nothing about Jimmy's neck problem. It was kept very quiet in the build-up to Rotterdam. There was a doubt about his fitness beforehand but the seriousness of the injury was kept very hush-hush and the few people who did know about it kept it a closely guarded secret. And when Jimmy hurt himself after just eight minutes it was a big shock to me and thousands of Villa fans to see 23-year-old Nigel Spink replace our former England international goalkeeper, with only a single league game to his credit in two years.

Having said that Nigel was more than able and a very good goalkeeper. He had all the attributes, ability, presence and temperament. He was also a very solid lad so none of us had any fears as he took his place between the sticks. Never the less it was a sensational substitution and, as all of football was about to discover, a sensational performance. We were under the cosh and Nigel was forced into action quickly, making a double save to deny Rummenigge. The same striker then went very close with an overhead kick but we got through to half-time 0-0. Klaus Augenthaler, the Bayern sweeper, was causing us immense problems with his breaks from the back, and I had to clear his goalbound header off the line after he nodded it past Nigel. I think it was midway through the second half before we tested their keeper when Tony Morley who had a long-range shot tipped over.

Then came the magic moment, the only one from that game. Tony Morley raced down the left flank, and twisted and turned into a position which was too acute for a shot. But somehow he managed to squeeze the ball across the six-yard box where Peter Withe had run. I swear Peter was no more than four feet from the goal-line but unmarked. He allowed the ball to run across his body and sidefooted it with his right foot, which was unusual for someone who was predominantly left-footed. It wasn't the cleanest of strikes and film of the game shows he almost missed but the ball struck the post and rolled over the line. The ball actually bobbled before it reached Peter because that particular six-yard box was very uneven. A scrappy goal but no one cared and now it's just a distant memory. Indeed it was a scrappy game but the most important thing was the result. No matter it was nowhere near a classic. No matter it wasn't the kind of football match that might have been expected between two very good teams. The records will always show the European Cup Final of 1982, Aston Villa 1 Bayern Munich 0. The record books won't show the freshness and the naivety, the tension of the underdogs winning against a team packed with German internationals.

Perhaps my most abiding memory of the night came when it was all over. All the celebrations on the field had passed and the champagne showers in our changing room had subsided and most of our players had showered and changed and made their way out to meet friends and family. I was probably the last one out of our changing area, maybe an hour after the final whistle, and as I walked out past the Bayern dressing room I noticed the door was ajar. So I thought I would pop in and see if anyone was still there to offer my commiserations and best wishes for the future, something like that.

Their changing room looked deserted but then I noticed a bag, then a foot next to it as I pushed the door a little more open. I pushed my head a fraction around the door and blow me down if I didn't see Paul Breitner, nearest to me, and next to him Karl-Heinz Rummenigge and both of them were sitting with their elbows on their knees and their heads in their hands. And because I never knocked they still had that look, a look I would never forget. It was a look of desolation.

I remember thinking that here they were, two of the biggest names in world football. And that's one of the reassuring things about football. Despite their stature and trophies they had won, international players of the highest order, they could still be reduced to desolation having been slain, reduced to mere mortals, flesh and blood. We were led to believe they were on absolute fortunes to win that day. We scooped £1,500 apiece before tax but who cared.

I actually felt, seeing their faces, how very fortunate I was and we were. So for it to hit them like that made a big impression on me.

The trophy also made a big impression when we got back to our hotel and we filled it with champagne. It was huge anyway but filled with champagne made it doubly difficult to lift. You had to tilt it carefully but the diameter of the rim was so huge and it must have had ten bottles of champagne sloshing about when it came to my turn to drink. I just remember having the most expensive shower in my life, Dom, Moet, Krug, Tattinger.

There are lots of memories that emerge when I cast my mind back to 1982. That night in Rotterdam was obviously the high point of my career as a professional footballer but something happened as we headed back to Amsterdam, a far more poignant memory that sits alongside altogether more enjoyable ones.

It was the time of the Falklands War and news reports from the South Atlantic were thrust out, 24/7, from the media. The day before the European Cup Final, 25th May 1982, news came through that HMS *Coventry* had been sunk, so, much of our thinking was for the service personnel thousands of miles away from where we were to play a football match. Then, as we were still on a high from lifting the trophy, we heard a news bulletin revealing that 19 sailors had been killed when the *Coventry* went down. It went very quiet. It didn't seem appropriate for us to be celebrating when families back home were in mourning. It put everything in perspective and certainly doused the atmosphere for the rest of the journey back to our hotel.

Some years afterwards Aston Villa sent me a DVD of the final and to this day I have never watched it because, one, it's an indulgence and two, I was more intrigued years ago than I am these days. I may sit down and watch it some day but I have had no desire nor appetite to watch for any reason other than nostalgia but I feel nostalgia can sometimes be a handicap. I'm more interested in tomorrow than yesterday.

There are many legacies from Aston Villa's European Cup win in 1982 but I doubt there are many relating to socks. After I had been at Thomas Telford School for about a year I received a call from a chap who said he was a big Villa fan and he wanted to ask me a favour. He didn't want to ask me over the phone asking instead to come and speak with me. I pushed him for a bit of a clue and he said, "I want you to come to a wedding." I got even more curious when he said he would pay me. Getting paid to go to a wedding was a new one on me so I was intrigued.

We met up and he explained that he was best man at an upcoming wedding and the bride was a lifelong Villa fan who had been to the 1982 European Cup Final with her father. After the final whistle when I was throwing my kit into the fans one of my socks landed on this girl's head. Apparently I was her favourite player and the best man explained that the father wanted to surprise his daughter by reuniting me with my sock, at her wedding. I was offered a fee but declined so Lily and I travelled down to Devon for the wedding and at the reception, as the father was starting his speech I prepared to make my entrance. They stood me behind a curtain and I felt like Eric Morecambe, waiting to pounce on Ernie, before making my entrance.

The father's speech was fairly short and he began by saying what a wonderful daughter she was and how he had brought her up right, as a Villa fan. Then he recounted the story of when they had both attended the 1982 European Cup Final and how it had been the best day of his life and one of the best days of her life, barring that day. He told the story of the sock which his daughter had treasured ever since. He produced said sock with "and ladies and gentlemen here is that very sock". The entire wedding party fell about laughing as he waved the sock around then he announced that as a special present for his daughter they were going to reunite the sock with its original owner: "Ladies and gentlemen, Kenny Swain." I walked in and as I approached the top table the bride sat there laughing and giggling and then transfixed as we eyeballed each other from about 30 yards. I gave her a big kiss and she was so delighted and we stayed on for what turned out to be a very enjoyable evening.

Of course I am very proud of the two major winners' medals but was guilty of not keeping them safe and long after I had retired from playing an occasion arose when I wanted to check them out and couldn't find them. I doubt I had removed them from our house more than three or four times since winning them but despite extensive searching they could not be found. Very quickly the realisation dawned I would have to replace them. In the first instance I phoned the Football League and asked if a replacement championship medal could be struck. They said it was possible and said the cost would be around £700 plus VAT. I agreed to that and my next step was to contact my insurance company who agreed to foot the bill for replacement minus the excess, which was something like £50. But I couldn't get another medal struck until

I got a letter of authorisation from the Football League which I duly obtained and the league told me to take said letter into the jewellers, in Birmingham's jewellery quarter. I went to the Victorian offices where they dug out the die for casting a new medal and left that particular ball to start rolling while I went after a replacement European Cup medal. The championship medal was solid gold while the Uefa medal was gold-plated. The only other difference was in supplier. While the Football League had a single supplier Uefa was served by many different companies. However I managed to initiate that process and while waiting for my replacement medals I got on with the decorating.

At full stretch with a roller atop the step ladder I almost fell off when Lily came in and tossed some items onto the table, asking: "Are these yours?" The missing medals! My wife explained that the chap who had bought our previous house had learned that we had moved back into the Crewe area so, after a period of about eight years, there we were with this chap, a former policeman, knocking on our door to return my medals. The irony of the whole reunion with my medals was the fact he came across them, behind a wardrobe, where he was decorating, on a shelf and the two medals, nothing else, had slipped from the top of a box, onto the shelf, and there they remained for all those years. And for all those years, and two house moves, I never realised they were missing. Then, with everything organised to replace them, they turn up like that restored to their rightful place, reminders of back-to-back medal-winning seasons.

The European Cup-winning season was also notable for me by virtue of the fact I had the honour of skippering Villa when Dennis Mortimer was absent which, given his staying power, wasn't very often. It's very difficult to express the pride I felt. There we were, reigning league champions and chasing the European Cup and somebody thinks I can toss a coin, doesn't get much better than that!

I was also very proud of my level of consistency for Villa and I only missed four games in my time at the club until we got to 1982/83 but that consistency still didn't stop Doug Ellis referring to me as "our right-back Martin Swain". Martin was the *Express and Star* Villa correspondent and to my knowledge never turned out for the club nor won a league championship, European Cup or Super Cup. But it's those little idiosyncrasies that help keep one's feet firmly on the ground, not that mine ever left terra firma.

We went into 1982/83 as European champions and Super Cup winners but we didn't start like champions, losing our opening two games. Looking back at the poor pre-season we had I suppose the poor start to our league campaign should not have been the shock it was because we went to Germany in the summer and played three games, against Schalke, Dortmund and Bremen, and got turned over in all three games, before kicking a domestic ball in anger. Then it got worse when we went down to play Portsmouth in a testimonial match and lost a game in which I remember being turned inside out by the Pompey winger I was marking or not marking as it happens. Defeat only served to increase the pressure on Tony Barton.

I was starting to form an opinion that some of the players at Villa were getting a little bit above themselves. Ron Saunders had always run a tight ship but he also maintained a financially equitable approach towards player salaries. There may have been one or two on bigger wages but Ron tried to run everything on a level basis with nearly all the players getting very similar money. If you were one of the majority you could compensate by earning appearance money which could be a significant hike up to parity with the higher earners.

That was the pragmatic aspect of professional football, earnings. It was highly incentivised and as Villa were doing so well at the time the scope to vastly increase your weekly wages was huge. When we were in the top three we could easily double our weekly wage. Our incentive was something like £150 per point, in stages, if you were at the top so the top-up could be three hundred quid on top of a basic of circa £400. To put it into relative perspective the average UK weekly wage at that time was £147.

I'm not sure if that incentive-based earning scheme was a contributory factor towards the feeling I was getting that some players were getting above themselves. We had a good bunch of professionals who would play anybody for tuppence or two hundred quid, it didn't matter. But one or two of the squad began to test the water so to speak and approached Tony Barton. However the timing was a little suspect because by then Doug Ellis was back and running the club so those attempts to secure a better deal came up against formidable opposition. They also caused the stable ship that was Aston Villa to rock.

Tony Barton didn't have the same ideas as Ron so we started the season with disunity rearing its ugly head. We lost at home to

Sunderland, 3-1, and then were trounced 5-0 at Goodison Park in midweek. When I reported for training on Thursday Tony pulled me in and said he was contemplating making changes for Southampton on Saturday. I was planned as one of those changes and there was a young lad, Mark Jones, coming through who had been doing quite well. Tony also told me that Gordon Cowans would be dropped as well, so that made me feel a little better as I was in good company. Tony tried to cushion the blow by adding that nobody was doing well at that time, which we all accepted. As it turned out "Sid" Cowans retained his place while I was dropped. I took that as being the writing on the wall as far as my Villa future was concerned because I was 31 and Mark Jones was only 19.

Although Villa lost 1-0 at Southampton to plunge to 22nd in the table the re-jigged team won the next four games, with a rejuvenated Gordon Cowans banging in three penalties, to help the team climb to fourth place. Gary Williams even claimed the number two shirt for the home win over Luton so I slipped to third in the pecking order behind Gary and Mark so it really was curtains for me. I still had a year or two left on my contract but money was never an issue for me. The only thing that ever motivated me was being in the XI so I wondered what I should do. I was playing reserve team football, the World Club Championship was on the horizon but I wasn't going to be involved in that, so it seemed to me that circumstances were adding up to seeking pastures new.

I think a lot of the media, and the general public, don't really understand how powerful a motivation being in the starting XI is for a professional footballer. I honestly believe that to be as true nowadays, with players earning £50,000 a week and more, as it was back in my era.

There is a very powerful perception that footballers don't care whether they are in the team or not, because of the money they earn but I know they do care and the vast majority of them, deep down in their souls, want to be in the team. It's the esteem, the recognition, if you like, that they have earned that right to be in the side, the reward for competing for that shirt. I wanted my shirt but that wasn't my call and the longer I went without Tony's call the larger the writing on the wall appeared and the more a move away from Villa Park seemed likely, and desirable.

It was November 1982 and there was a European game ahead, against Dynamo Bucharest. I was included in the squad but not having played in the first team since 31st August I wasn't optimistic about making the team sheet for that one. But just around the corner, as I was playing with fellow first teamers who had also fallen out of favour and aspiring youngsters, in front of the proverbial man and his dog, was to emerge the most powerful influence on my football career.

Chapter 5

Brian Clough and Forest

My first encounter with Brian Clough came during the period at Villa when I was confined to the stiffs and out of the first team picture for six or seven weeks although it seemed longer. When Tony Barton said he was considering changes he added I wasn't the only one with the axe hovering but as it turned out I was the only change and that flattened me.

Everton featured again, as they did so often in my career. We were due to play a reserve fixture against them at Villa Park and Pat Heard, who had been at Everton before Villa, told me Howard Kendall, the Everton manager, would be at the game to watch me. At the time they had a young lad, Gary Stevens, playing at right-back, and although he had been playing in their first team for a few weeks Pat told me they wanted a bit more experience, hence Howard's presence at our reserve game.

Naturally I was tingling at the prospect of being watched by "my team" and maybe fulfilling the dream of pulling on that revered blue shirt. That feeling was tempered by the possibility that Pat was simply having a laugh. Never the less Howard was going to be there. In fact before kick-off that evening Tony Barton told me somebody was coming to watch me but as we were hardly on speaking terms, which was sad, I just mumbled "yes" under my breath and shuffled away. Looking back I regret that situation and my reaction to it and how bitter I felt. I'm sure there was no malice in Tony's decision to drop me but I couldn't see that at the time. Players don't because of a feeling of self-importance, not that it was how I felt then, it was just that I had given so much to Villa and helped them win the league and the European Cup and I felt, deep down in my soul, the changes he was making weren't appropriate, weren't taking us in the right direction.

Tony told me that this person, who he never named, wanted to speak with me and he wanted to ensure I wasn't dashing off after the match. I confirmed I would stay behind so afterwards Tony approached me and said that manager wanted to speak to me upstairs as soon as possible because "Brian Clough didn't want to hang around". BRIAN CLOUGH! I nearly fell off my seat. I turned towards Pat Heard and if ESP works he would have got my telepathic message, which read, "you lying b*****d".

As the name Brian Clough slowly began to register my mind was working overtime. I had never quite fancied working for him, because of his reputation, but with the kind of record he had I soon had a change of heart and couldn't wait to get upstairs. I got scrubbed up and made my way to the lounge where my wife was waiting for me.

There were quite a few wives and girlfriends up there, which was the norm at reserve games, and Brian came up to me almost the second I walked through the door. "Aye up Ken, where can we go and have a drink?" That took me aback as we were standing in the middle of a lounge with a huge bar. So, politely, I pointed out to him that "here is as good a place as any, Mr Clough". He continued: "It is Kenneth, isn't it?" I told him it was usually Kenny to which he replied: "What's on your birth certificate?" I said: "Kenneth." "Kenneth it is then," and the formalities were completed.

"What are you having?" he said. "I'll just have a half please." "You'll have a pint," he replied as he turned to introduce a chap who was with him. "This is my gardener Joe. Joe this is Kenneth, he's a full-back here at Aston Villa. He's the lad we came to have a look at." Brian turned to order the drinks but as soon as I told him Lily was with me he insisted she join us. "Aye up Lily. Lovely to see you, lovely to meet you." After he had given her a greeting kiss Brian asked if there was somewhere we could go for a chat. He also asked who the club secretary was, so I told him it was Steve Stride. He said: "Do you trust him, because I need to speak to him?" "Yes, I trust him with my life, he's a great fellah," I replied. Steve showed us to a room and we sat down and Brian got straight to the point.

"You know why I'm here, don't you?" I told him that Tony Barton had mentioned he wanted to talk about a loan deal. "That's right. Viv Anderson is injured, he's got a bad knee. He's going to be out for a month or two so we need some cover, immediately, and you would be ideal for us. You know what we're all about, don't you?" I nodded and he asked if I would like to go for a month. I was bubbling inside, with expectation which translated into me telling Brian Clough I was grateful for the opportunity, and "thanks a lot". I said: "It's better than being in Villa's reserves because at least I am in the shop window." Brian smiled as he said: "That's good then. You come along and we'll have a look at you, you'll have a look at us and let's see how it goes, for a month anyway." He then turned to Steve Stride and barked: "I've never done one of these loan deals before so Steven you'll have to advise me and hold my hand here and furnish me with all the necessary."

Brian sorted out the salary side of things with Steve which basically meant that Forest would pick up the wages for me, as paid out by Villa. The parent club would raise an invoice for the requisite amount and submit that to the club taking the player on loan. The only difference was that the player being loaned would go on to the bonus scheme at the club he was going to and, temporarily, leave the bonus scheme of the parent club. That was the financial side of things but in terms of football I was actually going from a team that had made a poor start to the season to one that was well placed.

I think that meeting was on the Tuesday night and as we parted Brian turned and said. "See you on Friday, you know where the ground is, don't you?" I nodded but asked him about the following day and training. "The lads are off tomorrow and they're in on Thursday but you don't need to come in, not a fit lad like you. You don't need training, we'll see you Friday." And he was gone.

I went over on Friday and the first player I met was John Robertson, who I had played against a few times. He introduced me to the rest of the lads, who were brilliant and I felt totally at home as soon as I walked in, it was heartening. Cloughie was great, as were the club staff, and it was a welcome change from Villa where my whole world seemed to have collapsed so soon after winning the European Cup.

I remember John Robertson saying to me. "F*** me, I always thought you were a Cockney, being at Chelsea." When I told him of my Scouse heritage he asked if I was a red or a blue so I confirmed being a Bluenose. "Oh, they're a funny lot them." I asked him what he meant. "I love playing up there. A couple of years ago we were at Goodison and at one point during the game someone went down injured so play stopped and the physio came on. I was standing in front of the Bullens Road Stand, on the wing, hands on hips, as you do, minding my own business and facing back across the pitch towards the players' tunnel. It was fairly quiet then all of a sudden this fellah shouts out 'Oye, Robbo,' and as I turned round, 'move over, I can't see the game yer fat b*****d'."

Brian Clough signed me, initially on a month's loan, because Viv Anderson had been injured just nine games into the season. I made my Forest debut, at home to Birmingham City, in early 1983, then played in every game through to late February but by then Viv was fit again and ready for a recall.

I settled in very quickly at Forest and began to play probably the best football of my career. I really enjoyed it because the stress levels had virtually disappeared. I was at ease with what I was doing and it resulted in relaxed performances.

I ended up staying for three months on loan which was the maximum allowed at that time before I signed a permanent contract and in that period we only lost two or three times and got into the top three or four. At the end of the first month's loan Brian told me he was going to need me for another month because Viv was still a fair way off being fit. I told him I didn't have a problem with that but I was really looking for a permanent move. He rubbed his chin with his thumb and forefinger and said: "Look, why don't you come for another month. I think we like what we see." In fact I remember he said something to that effect in the team meeting that Friday. All the players were there and Brian announced: "We've got Kenneth for another month and if he's as genuine as he appears we might try and sign him because I think he might be a good addition to our squad."

I signed for another month and when that ended he said if I agreed to a third month he promised we would sort out a deal. He said he wanted to make the move permanent but there were obviously certain things that needed sorting out, not least: "What do they want for you?" I couldn't answer that question so I went back to Tony Barton who confirmed he had spoken to the chairman Doug Ellis on that very subject. When Tony said Villa wanted a hundred grand for me I was gobsmacked. A hundred thousand pounds for a 31-year-old was a bit steep considering I had joined Villa for that amount. When I told Brian Clough his reaction was what I expected: "A hundred grand for a f****** 31-year-old who's shot?" After we both laughed and calmed down a bit Brian said they would try and come to some agreement but that I would need to have another month at Forest, adding: "We can write in financial incentives based upon the loan spell." When I asked "was that per month?" he said "cheeky b*****d" but agreed.

All I had to do was spend a third month on loan, which I was more than happy to do, with the word of Brian Clough that a permanent transfer would be sorted for me at the end of the loan. "You do want to join us, don't you?" he asked. I think it was a rhetorical question because I was chomping at the bit with the prospect of turning a very enjoyable temporary transfer into a very enjoyable permanent one. However, there as an awful lot to sort before I became a Nottingham Forest player and most of it centred on Doug Ellis.

I have enormous admiration for what Doug did for Aston Villa after he returned. He kept the club afloat and gave it some status and ran a pretty tight ship but it is obviously other aspects of his nature that I, and others, call into question. And it was his part in the protraction of my permanent move to Forest that really upset me. The fee Villa wanted and what Brian Clough was prepared to pay were miles apart but there were a couple of other issues as well.

As European Cup holders we were due to play in the World Club Championship, early in 1983, and I was really looking forward to that, as a first team player. There was a financial incentive for us on the back of such a prestigious event. I think Toyota, who were sponsors of the game, had guaranteed Villa something like £90,000 for playing. I thought I was entitled to something for all the effort and contribution I had made in getting Villa into the European Cup and winning it, but football doesn't work like that.

Being out of the side, whoever was replacing me would be in line for that incentive and I felt that wasn't right, so I initiated negotiations to try and get the best kind of settlement I could to enable me to leave Villa but Doug Ellis would not budge. In addition to that issue there was also the matter of a loyalty bonus, around £5,000 a year, and on a lesser level there was my company car. It was all very messy but it became a kind of tit for tat barter scenario whereby one side would suggest withdrawing one aspect of their demands in return for a concession by the other side and vice versa. But the bottom line was they were unable to come to any satisfactory agreement because Doug was digging his heels in, which was what he did over most things, and it left me with the overwhelming feeling it was never going to get off the ground.

I passed on all the details to Cloughie and he told me to leave it with him which was reassuring. He engaged in negotiations with Tony, directly, but soon came to the same conclusion as I, with a few well chosen expletives, at a ridiculous situation. Brian then told me we were going to meet, myself, Tony Barton and himself to try and thrash out a solution.

What a fascinating meeting it turned out to be. The three of us sat, drinking tea, and the entire proceedings conducted by Brian Clough was a joy to experience. I was in the presence of two managers, one newly appointed and the other a manager with immense experience and a personality to match. It underlined for me how inexperienced someone could be despite the position they occupied, which is not meant as a slight on Tony. I was piggy in the middle trying to make sense of it all and hoping for some kind of satisfactory conclusion.

After one of those eerie silent spells that can often punctuate any conversation Brian looked Tony directly in the eye, and began to speak. "Look Tony, I can't see all of this being a problem. You want to sell the player, yes? I wanna buy him, yes? And the boy wants to leave you and joins us, yes? I can't see why we cannot do a deal."

It took less than ten minutes and it was handshakes all around. Tony obviously had some brief from Doug as to how low he could go and Brian made most of the concessions. Basically we all had to compromise, Cloughie had to pay a bit more, I had to accept a bit less and Villa had to settle for less than they wanted. It left me with a lesson for life, the basic principle of a club wanting to sell, a club wanting to buy and a player who wants to move from one to the other. It should be unproblematic, except for allowances that need to be made for individual factors. And I think a simple situation has become more exacerbated these days with agents and other people getting involved.

Anyway, there was me thinking it was all sorted but then the whole deal stalled and I think it was over something as insignificant as the car or something equally minor. I was so frustrated I told Tony Barton: "That's it, I'm staying." I could have sat out the remainder of my contract, which is something that is more likely these days than it was back then, but I telephoned Brian over the weekend to tell him of Villa's intransigence and that I was going back. He didn't respond with any advice or suggestions, it was almost a case of acceptance, however reluctant. When I reported for training on Monday I saw Tony and informed him if it wasn't settled I was going to call their bluff and stay, indeed I was so angry I WAS going to stay.

I got changed and with the rest of my Villa team-mates we jogged around Bodymoor, with Roy McLaren. We had just completed one circuit around the perimeter, and were just about to turn into a second lap but amidst the usual banter my mind was drifting. I had left those close friends and spent three months with Forest so, in essence, I had left them behind and moved on to new bunch of team-mates and my allegiance was with them, no disrespect to the lads I was jogging with at that moment. It was slowly sinking in that what I was doing wasn't right. I was doing the wrong thing and whatever my motives were for digging my heels in my gut instinct, as I ran, was me trying to prove something, which I thought was so futile. The realisation was "I don't want to be here. I want to be there". I didn't care what it was that was standing in the way I literally just peeled off from the group and as I ran off in the opposite direction I turned and said back to them: "That's it lads, I'm off. I'm going to Forest, see you." Out of courtesy I told Roy I was going and went in, got changed and that was it. That was my seminal moment. I don't know where Tony was, I jumped in the company car and went home and rang Cloughie to tell him I would be over for training in the morning.

I think I had basically come to the conclusion that to be with a club requires 100% commitment, the same I felt at all my clubs, looking back. When I returned to Villa, in a strop, it wasn't 100% and it dawned on me I could not do that. My commitment was tested and I found it wanting so I had to make the decision I did and join Nottingham Forest. The move certainly wasn't financially motivated because I was actually going to be on less money although there were bonuses and incentives at the City Ground because that's the kind of club Forest were, more incentive-based. I didn't have to move house so that was a plus because my two boys were at school. In fact I asked the boss if he wanted me to move over. He said: "Do you want to move over, where are your kids?" I told him they were at school and when he said "you don't want to move them do you?" I said not really. I only asked the question because most clubs wanted their players near to hand. He told me to stay where I was if I wanted to, adding: "And don't let any fool like me try to convince you to do anything different when your kids are settled." He then asked me if I could commute over from Solihull so I said it only took me just over an hour. He responded: "Now I couldn't do that, drive an hour, hour and a half every day to work and back again. I only live in Derby, which I know is only down the road, but I couldn't do that. But if you can and are happy where you are, you stay put." So I did. It was never an issue as I was comfortable driving across with no disruption to family life. Decision made, I left it to the clubs to sort out the finer points and the deal was done, an 18-month contract with an option for a further year at the end.

I had done well during my three-month loan but once Viv was fit it presented Cloughie with a dilemma. Viv was first choice right-back and one of the best in the country and the manager had me in that position. I guess it was a mark of how I had won my spurs, with Brian, but also a measure of how accepted I was at Nottingham Forest, that the manager saw it as a dilemma. It was actually at Old Trafford, before kick-off against United, when Brian, with his assistant Ronnie Fenton, pulled me into the corridor. Brian pointed his finger at me, which was what he always did to emphasise the point he was about to make. "Now then Kenneth, where do you want to play today, right-back or left-back?"

My mind was racing because Viv had played a couple of reserve games and was ready. But I was doing particularly well, as good as I had played in the loan period, so I told Brian I would prefer to play right-back because that was where I felt most effective. "Okay" was his abrupt response. He did an about turn and shot back into the dressing room and announced "same team as last week", which meant he had considered putting me somewhere else if I had agreed to play in another position to accommodate Viv's return, but it was a real vote of confidence that he had enough faith in me to keep me in at right-back instead of an England international. I remember thinking "bloody hell he prefers me". I knew Viv was going to come back somewhere but the only question for me was, being on loan, where did I stand?

Anyway, we lost at Old Trafford, 2-0, but in those days it wasn't the fortress it became and you could go there confident that you could maybe get a point and even a win wasn't as uncommon as it has been under Fergie. But what that particular defeat did was trigger off a sequence of poor results for us, nine without a win, which saw us slump to tenth and early in the run was the game at Birmingham.

The build-up to that game, and it was by no means out of the ordinary, was that we trained on the Wednesday and as I left for home Brian shouted across to me, "see you Saturday", which he often did to his players. So I sat at home in Solihull, the rest of Wednesday, Thursday and Friday wondering what the hell to do, in between going for runs in Dorridge Park, to keep fit. It wasn't a case of "oh he'll take care of himself", it was a simple fact that at Nottingham Forest we didn't train an awful lot and when we did it was short and sharp, never ever physical and Brian was always there, for every single session.

It was obviously a transitional period for Forest when I arrived. Trevor Francis had gone, Peter Shilton had gone to Southampton and Viv Anderson would soon be on his way to Arsenal. "Bas" Birtles had also gone to Old Trafford but returned just as I arrived at the City Ground.

It never really worked out for Garry at United so he was welcomed back into the Forest fold by Cloughie. I was always wary about players going back to a former club, wondering if it's ever possible to rekindle what was there before. But Garry was really at home once he returned to the City Ground. He enjoyed his football again. I don't know why it worked for him under Cloughie but not Fergie. Going to a club like United brings with it pressure and it has to be part of a player's personality, his character, that he's got to be able to face up to pressure. The pressure of expectation when running out in front of 45,000 as it was then or 75,000 as it is now means you have to be a bit more than just a bloody good footballer and a hard worker. And maybe that's why it didn't work out for Gary at United, I don't know.

Brian bought Ian Wallace, Johnny Metgod, Trevor Christie and Gary Megson in his efforts to change things around but he also had a few older players like myself, Paul Hart, Ian Bowyer and Colin Todd, lads who had been there a few years.

Whatever the playing personnel Brian was very demanding of his players and we would train with him watching on as we played at full steam, which was very much the way we played in matches. Ahead of the game at St Andrew's I spoke to Ian Bowyer, who was team captain, on the phone, and as we chatted he said I might find myself moved across to left-back against Blues to accommodate Viv. That's exactly what happened, and it never bothered me a jot. We went into the dressing room at Birmingham and Brian said he wanted me to "play left-back today" so Viv regained his number two shirt and I donned number three. Brian turned to me and said: "You know what Kenneth, you could end up being the second best right-footed left-back I've ever f*****g had." I asked who was the first. "Frank Clark," he replied. "But you've got to go some to beat him. He was the best right-footed left-back I've ever had. I would also have to add, unless you can play the guitar better than him."

I think Frank must have serenaded Brian on many an away trip and during my time at Forest he was always lamenting the parting of the ways when Frank went into management. When Forest would be at some hotel or other, for an away game, Brian would bemoan anyone who would listen. "Can't anyone play a musical instrument in here? Have we got no talent in this club?" It was normal for Brian to be drawn to a piano if the hotel we were staying at had one because he loved his music. Not that he could play the piano but he used to love sitting down at one. So I knew it was a hard act to follow, being a right-footed left-back but only the second best.

Forest hadn't had the best of starts to that 1982/83 season but things began to pick up after my loan spell was extended. We went through November unbeaten and climbed to third but a 3-2 defeat at Notts County dropped us down a couple of places, then three wins on the bounce saw us reach what would be our highest position that campaign, second. Unfortunately a 3-1 reverse at Everton meant starting 1983 on a downward spiral. In a dozen games from the start of the year we only won one, 1-0 at home to West Ham, and it was the home win over Everton at the start of April which began a run of nine games unbeaten, seven of them victories, that took us up to a final place of fifth. I could not explain the improvement and looking back at the records the only real change in terms of team selection was the arrival of Hans Van Breukelen. He took over from Steve Sutton for the third and fourth defeats in a run of four that immediately preceded that late unbeaten run. It was a run that earned qualification for the Uefa Cup.

Towards the end of my first Forest contract Brian offered me the extra year, with a signing-on fee that was about right for me at that age although it was exactly the same as what I was on, but when I spoke about that with him Cloughie simply said: "Why should we pay you more money, you're a diminishing asset. You're not getting better, you're actually getting worse."

Anyway I thought it better to get the season out of the way so left it until around the time of our final game. I went to Brian's office and saw Bobby Gould emerging but thought no more about it. We had finished the league programme but we had a Nottingham County Cup Final against Notts County the following midweek. It was FA Cup Final week and I got a call from Bobby Gould. He said he didn't know if Brian had spoken to me but said Coventry had made an offer for me. I said "right" and Bobby informed me Forest had accepted the bid. Bobby added: "I'd like to talk to you anyway and as you live quite close to Coventry it shouldn't be a problem, should it?"

Bobby said he knew that Forest had offered me a one-year contract and Coventry were offering two years at the same wages I was on at the City Ground. He suggested we meet on Cup Final day for an hour or so then shoot off and watch the game.

I think it surprised Bobby when I told him it was all news to me. He responded by offering me the captaincy at Highfield Road and assured me I would be good for Coventry and they would be good for me at that stage of my career. But the truth of the matter was I didn't really want to go no matter how attractive he made it.

I had to bide my time and was itching to talk to Brian about the whole affair. But when I finally pinned him down there was no discussion, no negotiation. He had made me an offer to stay, another club had come in and it was down to me. The setting was hardly conducive for discussing my future, the players' bath. Cloughie was first in, as usual. I asked him if I could have a word after and he said "yes". But before

I could get another word out Brian went on: "Did Bobby Gould ring you over the weekend? Hell of a nice man, Bobby. He came into my office the other day and nearly drank me dry. He never shut up about you Kenneth. So I thought 'put your money where your mouth is'. He offered me 25 grand, which is everything we paid for you, and it seemed a good deal to me because we've had a good stint out of you and got our money back and he's obviously desperate to speak to you."

We then adjourned to Brian's office so I could disclose what Bobby and I had spoken about. I told Cloughie we hadn't spoken in depth but the basic deal was for two years. All Brian kept on saying was "yes, yes, yes" as if he was waiting for me to tell him my decision. Then he changed tack and asked if I was going. I told him I wanted to stay. We shook hands and he smiled as he said: "Nice to have you back on board Kenneth." So, it had been a test. He gave me the option to leave and whatever the security and attraction of Coventry I really wanted to stay and I think Cloughie acknowledged that kind of loyalty, which he regarded as commitment. He still wouldn't better the deal he had offered me but that was the way he was.

Twelve months later I was out of the side and Brian had brought in another full-back, an Aussie lad, Alan Davidson, who was signed after a trial period and was playing instead of me. I thought that was curtains for me and that position was confirmed one night when Ronnie Fenton rang to tell me Portsmouth had been in touch and Alan Ball wanted to talk to me, adding: "Brian asked me to call you just to mark your card." All I could think was "he's done it again and not said a word to me".

Portsmouth were doing really well at the time and had been promotion contenders for a couple of years and Alan Ball was a player I worshipped at Everton so it was appealing. Alan called me and invited me down to Fratton Park to discuss a possible move. I went and we talked and it became an even more attractive proposition when Alan said they would pay me more than I was earning at Forest and there was a two-year contract on the table plus a signing-on fee.

It was what Alan Ball said to me about the football that really made up my mind. He said: "We have done very well over the last couple of seasons but I think with your experience to add to the mix we might just push it that little bit further because we have a lot of young players."

They did indeed have some cracking players, and characters. There was Kevin O'Callaghan, Kevin Dillon, Mick Kennedy, Mickey Tait, Vince Hilaire and Mickey Quinn would eventually come. So it was a very attractive situation and one to consider very seriously. When I returned to Forest and had just played in a reserve game Cloughie asked how it had gone down at Pompey. I told him very well and after speaking with Alan Ball and the chairman they had offered me a deal, which they wanted me to sign ASAP. I outlined the deal in detail and Brian agreed it was a really attractive package. I told him I was very interested and it was the truth. The deal was good and I seemed to be going nowhere in the Forest reserves. But I was dealing with Brian Clough and I guess I should have expected what he said next: "Here's what I think Kenneth. Why don't you get back in our f***** team?" I smiled rather sarcastically and told him I would if I could but "you pick the side". "Well, how 'bout you get back in our team and settle down again." I thought to myself: "He's agreed to me leaving then turned around and challenged me to get back in the team that he picks." Next day, I found myself back in the side and even more confused because Alan Ball was waiting for me to call him with my decision. Then Alan called me to find out what was going on and all I could tell him was I was back in the team and Forest wouldn't let me go anywhere, I was stuck.

It was history repeating itself and Cloughie had done me, again. So I just got my head down and got on with playing my football, in the first team, and enjoying doing so. But I couldn't lose the nagging feeling that the chance was gone, never to return. I should have had more faith because when the season ended Alan Ball did come back in for me and on the same terms. All financial terms would be written into the contract so everything would be clear to all parties. Cloughie then decided he wanted a fee for me and despite me thinking it might scupper the deal he convinced me that if Forest got a fee he could make an *ex-gratia* payment to me, which was perfectly legal, everyone would be happy and the deal could go through. It was all sorted and I would complete my move to Portsmouth FC to play for Alan Ball but there was an awful lot of water to flow down the Trent before that happened.

Forest could not have had a tougher start to 1983/84 and although we beat Manchester United 2-1 at Old Trafford we drew at Villa and lost to Southampton and Liverpool, and slumped to 15th. However, consecutive wins against QPR, Norwich and Luton lifted us up to seventh and put us in good heart for a piece of history, the first live First Division game to be broadcast, away to Tottenham on 2nd October.

It was a Sunday game so we met, as usual for any game down south or in London, at the Crick Post House which was just past where the M6 joined the M1. I had just taken delivery of a brand new Ford XR4i, GTX, and lots of other letters which I can't remember, all singing, all dancing Starship Enterprise type, in gleaming white. It was a real eye-catcher or so I thought, a real expression of the big time. God knows what I looked like. Thinking back, it beggars belief.

My wife was driving it and was dropping me off to catch the team bus. It was a baking hot day and just as we were about to turn on to the motorway I looked left from the passenger seat and thought "bloody hell" as I spotted bottle-necked traffic as far as the eye could see. We had no choice but to filter into three lanes of stop-start momentum and I was just grateful that we were half an hour early although I could have walked faster than we could drive. Cars breaking down on the hard shoulder didn't help as the spare time we had slowly eked away towards worry. I sat there twiddling my thumbs as we edged forwards, nose to tail, still a mile short of the meeting place. All of sudden there was a 'whoooosh' in my left ear as this blur shot past us, on the hard shoulder.

The blur turned out to be the Forest team bus with driver Albert's foot firmly flooring the accelerator. I shouted to Lily to pull out and follow the coach but she couldn't because we were wedged in. So I began banging the horn in a vain attempt to get understanding British motorists to allow us to pull in front of them. "Surely they wouldn't want me to miss the team bus on its way to a top First Division fixture, yeh, right." Then I saw the bus's brake lights come on as it screeched to a halt, still on the hard shoulder, due to the broken-down cars. I thought "quick, this is my chance". Lily pulled on to the hard shoulder and we sped in pursuit of our bus but then we had to stop again, too many broken-down cars. Then the coach pulled back onto the main carriageway and we had to try and follow suit.

The cat and mouse scenario continued for what seemed an eternity and I was getting more and more stressed. I even tried to take over the driving but progress was impossible. We were so near yet so far then I thought "b******s, I can run there". So, bag in hand, a tracksuited Forest full-back jumped out of the car and sprinted down the hard shoulder in hot pursuit like an extra in *Chariots of Fire*. I got to within 300 yards or so and was encouraged to see the brake lights come on again. "I can make it, I know I can," I thought as I closed the gap. Just then the coach pulled out again and back on to the hard shoulder not far away from the exit.

There was no way I was going to make it so I decided to climb up the embankment and cut across the fields to the hotel. There was still no sight of the coach because we hadn't reached the brow of the hill which was just before the slip road. At the top of the embankment I couldn't see the coach at the hotel so I panicked, thinking I had missed it. I had two choices; race down the motorway and wait at the junction, in the hope I could intercept the coach, or run to the hotel and if the coach emerged I could dog-leg and meet it. I decided on the latter and by the time I reached reception I was covered in sweat.

I asked if the coach had been and the receptionist said no one had and no one had asked for me, bearing in mind those were the days pre-mobile phones. Panic had now set in. I had to get back to where I had left Lily and the car, quickly, because I had told her if I wasn't standing there I would have made the coach so she was to head home. So I sprinted back across that same field but by the time I had reached the fence I was horrified to see the traffic flowing again. "NO COACH, NO WIFE" thoughts bombarded my head as I sat on the fence, head in hands. Then I thought I could be watching the game, live on television, back at the hotel with a pint in my hand. Then a shaft of sunlight as I saw a white Ford XR4i and my frantic waving was spotted by Lily who pulled over. I bundled her out of the driving seat and floored the accelerator and pointed the car south.

Reaching 110mph down the M6 and the briefest of explanations to Lily as to why she could look forward to an unexpected trip to North London instead of feet up at home reading the Sunday papers. More panic ensued with the fuel needle in the red zone, top-up required so I pulled into Watford Gap Services. While Lily fuelled us up I got on the phone to her brother Billy, who lived in North London. I asked him to meet me on the North Circular and explained my dilemma. I told him to ring Tottenham and try and get through to the changing area, a little later, and try and speak to Cloughie or any of his staff and make sure he told them I was delayed but on my way.

More warp-factor driving got us to the designated meeting point from whence Billy, driving like a cabbie doing the Knowledge, weaved through the traffic to get us to White Hart Lane. Less than an hour before kick-off I dashed in, sweat-soaked tracksuit clinging to my breathless body, and burst into the away dressing room, by which time some of our lads were already changing. "Eh up Kenneth, where the f***** hell have you been?" said Cloughie. "Where the hell have I been, bloody hell, I was at the junction…" "But you weren't at the bloody hotel when we stopped," interrupted the manager. "No, I wasn't, I was actually half an hour in front of you …" "You weren't at the hotel when you should have been," he interrupted again. "No but I was in the same traffic jam you were and the next thing I see was Albert's bloody Nigel Mansell impersonation whizzing past me. So I jumped out of my car and was legging it towards the coach. I managed to get within a few hundred yards before Albert floored the pedal, again."

A short period of silence followed, ended by Cloughie, quizzical look on face. "That wasn't you running up the hard shoulder was it? I see now. Actually the lads were shouting down from the back seat 'hey boss, Swainey's coming up the hard shoulder' but I simply asked how many we had on board. Thirteen was the head count so I said f*** it we've got enough. Only kidding, are you fit?" "Half a stone lighter but I'm f***** fit." "Get stripped, you're playing. Relax, you got here, that's the main thing. Now then, are you going to have a drink with me, what do you want?"

I decided a brandy would be appropriate so Brian asked Ken Smales to procure drinks for us, stipulating a Scotch for himself, ending his request, as he always did, with "kind sir". So Ken disappeared into the bowels of the stadium, reappearing, five minutes later, empty handed, to report he couldn't find anywhere to get the drinks to an incredulous Cloughie. "You can't find a f***** bar at Tottenham Hotspur, White Hart Lane? They've got more f***** staff than we've got crowd. Go f***** try again, they must have more bars here than the West End." We eventually got our drinks, supped up and got on with the business of a big game.

We lost 2-1 after leading 1-0 at the interval through Colin Walsh. Gary Stevens equalised and when it looked like we were on for a point Mark Falco got the better of Paul Hart and headed goalwards. The ball was just about to cross the line when Steve Archibald got a toe on it. Harty, like any defender when beaten, took it very personally, but he was a top player. I had played against him a few times when we were at Villa and Leeds respectively and we became friends so we were quite close when he joined Forest. But he always operated under the handicap of bias from the manager because of the bad time Cloughie had during his 44 days at Leeds, so he always had it in for Paul although he was a player who gave Brian exactly what he wanted, a tall, commanding centre-half like he always went for such as Larry Lloyd or David Needham, but he still gave Paul a dog's life. He often had a go at him after games blaming him for this, that and the other, poor defending, the state of the economy. If something was wrong it was Harty's fault usually accompanied with: "You might have taken your old f****** club down but you're certainly not taking my club down." That was also the backdrop to another game against Spurs.

I think we were a couple of goals down and one of them was a particularly poor goal, from a defensive perspective, a header at a corner. So after trooping in at the break we all sat there, fearful of looking up and making eye contact with Brian who was aiming his observations at individual players in his own inimitable style. Then he got to Paul Hart. "And you, what the f****** hell were you doing at that corner?" pointing his finger at Harty. "What was I doing? Didn't you see him?" "See who, see what?" replied Mr Clough. "Didn't you see him? He (Falco) pushed me." Rolling his eyes Cloughie took up the plea, sympathetically, not. "He didn't, did he?" he said, staring directly at Paul who was looking distinctly hang-dog. So Brian walked closer to Harty, put his hand on his shoulder and turned to the rest of the team. "Hey lads, did you hear that. Blow me. Mark Falco has pushed him. Can you believe that?" And in the blink of an eye he was back to addressing our shrunken violet centre-half, adding: "Well next time f****** push him back and keep that f****** ball out of my f****** net."

But Cloughie wasn't averse to bigging Paul up either. He would say: "Eh, Harty, I haven't seen that for years. You stood out there like a f****** lighthouse. I've never seen a centre-half yet bring the ball down on his f****** chest and stroke a pass out with his weak foot, in the middle of our penalty box under that kind of pressure. I haven't seen that for years. That was absolutely brilliant young man."

I doubt there has ever been a better psychologist in the game, certainly not one I have encountered, but he did give away occasional clues to his intentions, whether by accident or design. With hindsight it was definitely the latter as perfectly illustrated by the pre-match meal routine on a Friday.

We were away to Arsenal and on the Friday after training we had our usual team meeting and were sitting there waiting for Cloughie, who bowled in, squash racquet gripped firmly in hand. "Sorry I'm late lads," he said as he sat down and ordered the steward to get the drinks in, making sure everyone was sorted. That's how laid back it was under Brian, more a social gathering than a team meeting. After some general chit-chat about what we had watched the previous evening on television we eventually got on to the subject of the following day's fixture, after a fashion.

What little we had done in training was mentioned in passing, it was that informal, and the only upping of the ante was when Brian raised his voice a couple of notches to exclaim: "And by the way it's about time we got a f****** result down at Arsenal because I don't know what it costs us when we go down to these away games Ron (Fenton). We've got our own coach and we've cut our cloth accordingly but we stop in hotels and that must set us back £800 or whatever. Well, I've thought, whenever we go down to Arsenal we usually come back with a kick up the pants, we certainly don't come back with any points, and we always end up light in money with those trips so we won't be stopping for a pre-match meal tomorrow lads, we'll be having soup and sandwiches on the coach instead but it won't be just any soup and sandwiches. You can have anything you like, Marks and Spencer's, Cross and Blackwell, f****** Heinz, you name it, you can have the best so what's it to be, 'cos you can't have everything." So then there was a bit of a culinary exchange as the lads told him what soup they wanted before he added: "And we'll have an assortment of sandwiches. That way if we come back tomorrow with f*** all, which is how we normally come back from Arsenal, it won't have cost us anything to come back with f*** all."

We were on that soup and sandwiches lark for a good while and when we were on the coach eating the sandwiches he would often sidle up to an individual player and whisper, "Hey, go steady, not so many sandwiches," or something similar, which was a good indicator as to whether or not you were playing. On one trip, to Chelsea I think, Ronnie Fenton came to the back of the bus with a plate of sandwiches.

Hands dived in and Ronnie would urge restraint, "only have one", which was a good indicator that person was playing. He held the plate towards me and I declined, telling him I had already had one. "Go on Kenny, you can have a few more if you want," so it was a pretty strong hint I wasn't playing that day.

I have been fortunate in my career and rarely missed a game through injury, fortunate too in terms of consistency of appearances. I only missed one game in my first season with Forest and it was the same the season following but then came the day when Cloughie pinned up the team sheet and some of the lads crowded around for a first look and from within the scrum came a voice. "F***** hell Swasiney, about time, you're not playing, we were beginning to think you were his blue-eyed boy."

I walked over to the team sheet and sure enough I wasn't even sub. I was astounded because I thought I had played well the week before. Then I thought, "well, I didn't play badly". Then I began scratching my head to try and recall why he might have dropped me and remembered "well, I did have a stinker a couple of weeks back but have done ok since then". When it finally sank in I trotted off, tail between my legs, leaving the rest to change. Nobody made a big fuss about it, you were in or you were out, and I was out.

I was upset and went away wounded. I sat with my wife and a few other lads who were also surplus to requirements. Lily asked me why I wasn't playing and the answer was "I don't know". She said I ought to find out and I was fuming enough for it to seem a good idea at the time. I sat there stewing over half a pint and couldn't see any reason for being dropped. I couldn't let it go, at least that is what I had convinced myself.

I went over to Brian's office, where he always adjourned after pinning the team sheet up. I asked his secretary Carol where he was and when she confirmed he was in his office I asked to see him. Carol agreed to have a word. Meanwhile I sat on the chairs just outside the office with people milling around waiting for Cloughie to emerge. A few minutes later Carol appeared to tell me he was asleep, which is something he often did. I went back to the lounge, and another drink, with Carol's promise she would tell Brian I wanted to see him. I went back later, by which time it was well past 2.30pm. All of a sudden he burst out of his office and it was one of those occasions when he looked just like a lion. I don't know if that was because I felt like his next meal but he was loud and brazen. He didn't even make eye contact with me, in fact I'm not even sure he knew I was seated there. He barked out instructions to one of the commissionaires in between greetings here there and everywhere with "hello young man". He was personality with a capital P.

I couldn't help but wonder if he had really been asleep but then I thought "lions do that, don't they, before they jump into action and begin the hunt for a kill". Brian certainly had that aura about him so I was coming to the conclusion that it probably wasn't the best time to speak to him. I peeled off in one direction while he went in another, being polite to some, barking at others. I headed back to the lounge then, around 2.45pm, Alan Hill popped his head around the corner and beckoned me over, finger crooked. "You wanted to see the gaffer didn't you?" he said. I nodded and Alan said he would see me now.

I'm feeling like he's got me on the back foot and no matter how much I wanted to avoid the inevitable I knew I couldn't not turn up. I made my way over with my brain spinning, wondering all sorts. Alan marched me along the corridors and into the changing room, announcing "here he is boss" as Cloughie chatted away to a couple of players. "Eh up Kenneth, come here, come sit down by me." I did as requested and sat next to him, booted and suited, as some of the players were out on the pitch, others still changing. He tapped me on the knee. "Now then, you wanted a word with me. What's it about? Now, if it's about your missus, or the kids or there's a problem with the family I'd gladly talk to you. If it's anything else…" I mumbled something inane about it not being any of the above but he interrupted. "If it's about anything else, I've got nothing to say to you." Desperately trying to hang on to a rapidly disappearing opportunity I said I would speak to him after the game. Nice try. "I'm going to the theatre tonight Kenneth, can you believe it? Barbara is taking me. Me going to the f***** theatre? I don't often go out Saturdays but she's taking me there straight after the game. Unless you want to speak up now."

I mumbled something like a demented Norman Collier but basically he'd thrown the gauntlet down. As if I was going to take him on when he was so obviously up for the fight. I went off with my tail between my legs, again. That taught me a lesson but that was life with Brian, a litany of lessons. Life at Forest was never dull and we had a few surreal experiences as well including, for me, a repeat of the experience which happened at Villa when we lost at home to title rivals Ipswich. At Forest it centred on a Uefa Cup tie against Celtic.

It was an absolutely frozen evening for the first leg, at home, 23rd November 1983. As the City Ground is next to the river the mercury didn't need much encouragement to plummet. I remember driving over from Birmingham having been warned to get there early, half an hour earlier than normal. It was nothing to do with the weather but because we were taking on Celtic and their legendary support which is why so many testimonial games feature the Glasgow club. They can take tens of thousands to any game, let alone a European one.

As I neared the ground I seriously doubted if the game would go ahead because everything was frozen. When I arrived the place was swarming with Celtic supporters. There was green and white everywhere. I'd obviously heard so much about Rangers and Celtic and the colour was so vivid, it was an amazing spectacle that unfolded before me as I turned in to the car park.

I was even more certain the game would be called off when we went out to inspect the pitch because one half was frozen. When we trained the day before we thought that if there wasn't a sudden thaw we would not be playing. There was no thaw but amazingly the referee deemed it playable so there would be obvious problems with footing because one side of the pitch was softer than the other, which was frozen, thus presenting major difficulties for those who were playing down the middle. On the flanks you could anticipate one half of the 90 minutes as near normal as November would allow, on the other side it was Torvill and Dean.

So the game was always going to be a bit of a lottery but the vivid memory of that night was looking around the City Ground an hour before kick-off and the stadium being nearly three-quarters full, most of the fans in green and white, almost like uninvited guests. I looked up at the floodlight pylons that stood in the four corners and was stunned to see Celtic supporters dotted at varying intervals all the way up those pylons hanging on with gay abandon. They had flags or scarves in one hand and cans in the other with more being spilled earthwards than they were drinking. Having said that they were so well behaved it gave credence to a story I later heard about a Glasgow policeman who was in Nottingham for the match. Apparently he visited the local police and seeing reams of charge sheets being prepared in advance told the local force they wouldn't be needed. After the game they were forced to agree. There was a spill on to the pitch but that was down to sheer weight of numbers from the crowd of 32,000.

The result was 0-0, which in European terms was always a good result for the away team but the thing that stood out for us, and was a real deja vu moment for me, happened after the game. It had echoes of that crucial game Villa lost to Ipswich in the title-winning season.

The Forest lads were all a little disappointed but not Brian Clough. Never, ever, did he convey, by body language or words, any sign of resignation. I'm not saying he was always positive but whatever the result it was all water off a duck's back as far as he was concerned.

We were all in the showers or the bath and all we could hear from the Celtic dressing room was a raucous rendition of "It's a grand old team to play for". There was lots of banging and stamping to accompany the singing and at that point I remember thinking to myself: "I've seen this before, they think it's all over, but it's not." A fortnight later we set off for the second leg and if any one game typified Brian Clough and Nottingham Forest it was the match at Celtic Park on 7th December 1983, in every respect.

It was a real social occasion because Brian used to invite family members along. He would say: "By the way lads if your missus wants to come we'll pay for the air fare but you'll have to pay for the hotel, 50/50 so just give us a cheque for half the total cost." Lily came with me on that particular trip but it wasn't as straightforward for those players not married. There'd be whispered suggestions, by the younger players, that they would like to take a girlfriend but there was even quieter tut-tutting from the older players who said they didn't think it was a good idea to ask the manager that particular question. One or two did chance their luck and asked anyway but Brian's response was: "Your girlfriend, get f****** lost. When you're married you can bring her. When you've made the commitment you can bring her." Another point of principle on which Mr Clough held strong, intractable views was insisting we sit with our wives. If I tried to sit with the lads it would be a quick word from the manager: "Hey, Kenneth, Lillian, you two sit here," as he pointed to a couple of adjoining seats.

The Forest party met up at East Midlands Airport on the Monday morning where we boarded the plane for Glasgow. The gaffer was sitting just in front of me asking the stewardess, politely: "Excuse me darling, can we have a bottle of champagne please? No, go on, make it two." The glasses were then passed along the aircraft to the Forest group so we could all join in, players, staff et al. So en route to a European game we drank champagne at 30,000 feet, which was new to me.

We arrived at the airport and got on the coach waiting to take us to our hotel and it turned out the driver was a Rangers fan. As we drove through the city centre, heading for the Marine Hotel in Troon, we went through Paisley and Cloughie bent the ear of our driver seeking confirmation that Celtic manager David Hay owned a bar in the area. "Aye, Davy's bar, it's just around the corner." That was enough for Brian who said we'd pop in for a drink. When the driver said there was nowhere to park his coach the manager told him to drop us off and "bugger off" until he was needed and he could come back and pick us up.

So after a flight from East Midlands, liberally sprinkled with champagne, around midday we were in Davy Hay's bar with Brian Clough ordering our drinks; a couple of beers here, a few lagers there, a few shorts and, of course, a shot of Scotland's finest for him. Then off we went to the hotel where we sorted our room keys out, or tried to.

There were just two of us who took their wives on that trip. Hans Van Breukelen brought his wife, Karen, but we weren't sure what the arrangements would be when we got there so when it came to the rooming list it was something along the lines of Ian Bowyer and Peter Davenport, Kenny Swain and Mrs Swain etc. But when all the keys had been dished out Hans wasn't too happy and having discussed it with Karen he told me he thought we should room together and leave our wives to share a room, adding: "I think we should prepare like everyone else no matter what the boss says." Lily was happy enough with that but importantly Cloughie wasn't, as he indicated when the keys were being handed out.

"Well, you sleep with her at home don't you, what's the difference here? If you were at home together you'd sleep with her wouldn't you?" Of course we nodded in silent assent. "So what's the difference?" I suppose it was difficult to argue with that kind of logic.

We didn't do any training on arrival, we simply sat down for lunch and a bottle of wine wasn't long in arriving at the tables. That was usual for us before games anyway, white wine and red wine, the norm. We had our meal then it was "see you at dinner" from Brian and off we all went, our separate ways, at 3pm. I went to the room, fell asleep and that was it until we assembled for the evening meal and thereafter retiring for the night.

The next morning we all went for a walk, and we still hadn't seen a ball. Brian told us that there was a marina nearby so we walked about a mile up the coast to this yacht club, in blistering winds, and as soon as we smelled the appetising aroma Brian rubbed his hands, declaring "fish and chips, we'll have some of that". We sat down and he asked if they had any haddock. "We have the best haddock in the world here. It was swimming around out there nay so long back" was recommendation enough and the manager promptly ordered, "haddock and chips for me and give the lads whatever they want". So there we were, the day before going into the cauldron we knew awaited us at Parkhead, preparing with fish and chips and a pint. We had another drink before strolling back to the hotel and that was our build-up to a Uefa Cup tie.

Back at the Marine Hotel we whiled away the evening playing cards and dominoes in a sleepy seaside hostelry in a most calm and relaxing atmosphere. It was a stark contrast to all the newspaper and media hype that billed the game as "A Battle of Britain". We never ever felt any kind of pressure and that was all down to Brian Clough's approach. That was the way he was and that's how he played it. There wasn't any front about it, he genuinely approached any game, any situation, in that calm manner and that was somehow transmitted to the players. He took the sting out of everything. We would play cards, relax, watch television. There was no training and the game was the next day but that evening it was so relaxed, warmed by the alcohol and the crackling log fires. It was so relaxed that the hotel residents were winding us up with all kinds of banter which, when we were able to comprehend, would translate into "you lot are on a hiding to nothing tomorrow, lambs to the slaughter".

The next morning we went out on to the links in front of the hotel. Not on the actual course itself, just the grass verges, and Ronnie Fenton tossed us a ball. It was the first time we had seen one since the previous Saturday when we beat Leicester 3-2, to go sixth in the table. We just had a knockabout with the ball, a few keepy-uppies, nothing too strenuous for about half an hour. Then we had a couple of passing drills before heading back to the hotel, having seen neither hide nor hair of the manager, to get ready for the game. Lunch, a glass of wine followed by a kip in the afternoon and that was something that is a strong memory from that particular trip, being in bed two or three times having a sleep.

When we were on the coach heading for Parkhead the traffic was bumper to bumper, not that Brian noticed because he slept most of the way there but you could tell by the crowds it was a massive occasion. As our coach slowed down for the umpteenth time because of sheer volume of traffic I noticed a huge advertising hoarding on which there was a huge picture of a bottle of Bell's whisky named "afore ye go" which was the slogan on the bottle. At that precise moment Brian woke up, scratched the back of his head, looked at the hoarding and turned to our club secretary Ken Smales and said: "Ah Kenneth, just the job, I'll have one of them." So Ken poured him a Scotch which he was drinking as we pulled up at the players' entrance, having been escorted through the masses by mounted police.

We eventually managed to get through into the stadium and as we walked through the main entrance Jimmy Greaves was there in his role as a commentator for ITV. Jimmy and Brian obviously knew each other from their playing days and they greeted each other warmly and Brian gave Jimmy a great big hug and a kiss on the cheek which he often did, kissing me there loads of times. But then Brian, arm around Greavsie's shoulder, turned and pointed in the direction of Garry Birtles and Peter Davenport and announced: "England's best striker, ever. Not quite as good as me though Jim, were you? Couldn't beat my record could you?"

When it came time for us to take a walk on the pitch we just sauntered out and I don't know what it was, maybe the atmosphere, but we were really up for it. It was about an hour before kick-off and "The Jungle" as it was known then, at the side of the pitch where the Celtic supporters were closest to the pitch, was a bank of incessant whistling and jeering. There was a barrage of vitriolic songs, fuelled by ancient antipathy towards "ye Sassenachs" aimed directly at us. It was a very hostile atmosphere but it was one that made you want to stick your chest out and shout "bring it on".

We couldn't wait, to be honest, and that night we played them off the park. We won 2-1, Steve Hodge and Colin Walsh scored before Murdo MacLeod pulled a late goal back for Celtic to make it a bit of a ding-dong battle for the last ten minutes or so. Our young lads, especially Hodgey, Peter Davenport and Colin Walsh, were full of running and they couldn't match us. At the end of the game, and it's something you sometimes see at the top grounds, we had the spectacle of us being applauded off the pitch by the home supporters. It was an almost universal standing ovation from a sea of green and white, although there was a tiny pocket of a few hundred Forest supporters, which really added to the memory of a night to remember.

After the game I met up with Celtic legend Danny McGrain. At that time my youngest son, Iain, had just been diagnosed with diabetes and I was picking up information about that condition from anywhere and anyone I could. Having read about Danny being diabetic we spoke about diabetes and he gave me his shirt and told me to give it to Iain which was a lovely gesture from a lovely man. Before we left I popped in to have a drink with David Hay, my former team-mate from Chelsea. All in all it was a special trip from beginning to end with the quarter-final to look forward to next, but there was still the little matter of a five-way tussle for the league championship with Liverpool, Southampton, Manchester United and QPR.

Top-flight football was intense and, depending on how well you were doing, Saturday, midweek, Saturday was usually the order of the day as far as the playing schedule went. But Cloughie was always mindful of routine and keeping it, or breaking it, whichever he deemed appropriate. And if he made many of our away trips in Europe family affairs, he balanced things out by regularly arranging mid-season breaks for the players only.

Brian had a place in Majorca, Cala Major, and one day he announced that we were going away for a week after we played our Saturday fixture. It was my first experience of that kind of break and it was a new experience when Cloughie told us to tell our wives, "break it to them easy" because he was as conscious as we were that our better halves were never too keen on losing us for days at a time let alone a week. But at times like that he was quite smart. What he used to do was send us home after the game with a bunch of flowers and a big box of chocolates or he would have them delivered, while we were away, so he definitely kept the wives sweet.

Ever the pragmatist, I remember him saying to the players, about that trip to Cala Major: "Look lads, this trip is costing £190 a head and you can't expect a club our size to keep funding these trips so you buy the air fares and we'll take care of the hotel, food etc. So £90 from you and a hundred quid from the club, hands up who wants to go."

Some of the better paid players were reluctant because they felt if the club wanted to do all that they should be paying for it while the rest of us regarded it as nice to be able to get away to the sun for a week, especially in the middle of winter. Ninety quid was not that bad so it was a goer and early one Sunday morning we turned up at East Midlands Airport.

It was around the time of my birthday and as I settled into my seat the first of the small bottles of wine dropped in my lap, along with birthday wishes from the lads. Several bottles and more birthday wishes later I was as happy as a newt and conscious, as you are, that the alcohol was spreading warmly through my body. Then Cloughie appeared, plonked himself halfway along where the Forest party was seated and announced there would be a meeting after dinner, at the hotel, and then it was straight to bed before training tomorrow. Before adding: "And by the way Kenneth, have you had enough red wine to drink?" He never missed a thing.

That night at the hotel he was going on about training in the morning and making sure we would all be there on time, but Willie Young got the hump. Willie had come from Arsenal and he and Cloughie were always locking horns over something, though he did love Brian to bits and the feeling was mutual. But on that occasion he spoke out, in front of everyone. "F****** hell, first of all you're asking us to come out here for a break then you're asking us to pay half of it and now you're telling us we're f****** training."

Of course we had a few drinks when we arrived and Willie had managed to get himself in a spot of bother with one of the hotel residents so everything was in place for a major row when Cloughie turned up. He walked over to where I was sat and whispered: "Kenneth, what the hell are you doing sitting here with this lot at this time of night? You've got a lovely missus at home so what are you doing mixing with this f****** lot?" I hesitated from replying "they happen to be my team-mates" and we took the hint that it was time for bed.

The next morning we got up, had breakfast and turned up in our training gear but there was no sign of the manager. Being my first trip I was trying to catch my breath and so was Danny Wilson, who

I roomed with, because it was a completely different world to the one he had experienced in hundreds of games with Chesterfield. We stood there, stripped and ready for training and quizzed Bomber, the skipper, about what we were going to do and what the schedule was, and, of course, Ian hadn't a clue. Then Willie Young came down, still mumbling and complaining that we shouldn't be training, shouldn't be paying and "what kind of a club is this".

Brian turned up and in time-honoured Pied Piper fashion we trooped out of the hotel behind him. Within five minutes we were on the beach, off came the shoes and socks and Cloughie started paddling in the water. We followed suit and it must have been a strange sight to see a group of footballers paddling in the Med, shoes draped over shoulders, just enjoying a bit of banter. People were staring but when they recognised Brian Clough they eased themselves back into relaxed mode because they all knew him over there and nothing he did was strange anymore. Very pleasant it was too, warm sunshine for us while England was still in the grip of winter.

Of course we wondered when we were going to train. Willie was still complaining for Scotland, banging on about having to train, when we weren't, training that is. Suddenly Brian spotted John Toshack and shot off to have a chat with him, leaving us to our own devices so we started skimming stones on the sea or kicking up sand. That continued for half an hour and slowly it dawned on us that training was looking increasingly unlikely. Another half-hour elapsed before Cloughie returned. We set off back the way we came and Brian turned to Ken Smales and asked him to pop into a restaurant to ask if they could accommodate 22 of us for lunch. We had to wait half an hour so Cloughie got the drinks in and I'm sat there thinking this wasn't a bad way to spend time, eating, drinking and generally having a good time, at someone else's expense. The leisure lasted for three days before it suddenly kicked in that we had a game looming at the weekend. I had to get myself out running and it wasn't long before the rest of the lads joined in. We never saw a ball so running was how we trained.

Importantly Brian knew we wouldn't let ourselves, or him, down and we had enough good pros who would lead by example and the younger ones tagged along. Being mid-season the fitness was there anyway and it was simply a matter of topping up before heading back to England to spend the Friday evening in the hotel, round the corner from the City Ground. On the day of the game we didn't even get the coach. We walked from the Windsor Lodge, about half a mile, mixing and chatting with supporters on the way in what I guess was very much the way it had been in Brian's playing days.

Domestically season 1983/84 could best be described as inconsistent. We had four players who ended the season in double figures for goals scored; Garry Birtles, Peter Davenport, Colin Walsh and Steve Hodge, indeed we ended up as top scorers in the First Division with 76 goals, three more than eventual champions Liverpool. Unfortunately we let ourselves down by conceding 45. It was almost a case of "you score three and we'll score four". But Cloughie was a bit like Alex Ferguson in that he did tend to load up with attack-minded players, individuals who could win a game with a goal. It wasn't a case of loading up with strikers, more a case of having a goal threat in the team. Brian always had that threat in abundance as does Fergie today. Defenders can help you avoid defeat but goalscorers win you games. I remember during my brief sojourn into management Joe Royle told me: "Kenny, collect them, goalscorers, strikers. If there's one to be had and you have the money, collect them. Strikers are always worth it because you can always sell them." It was something Dario Gradi also instilled in me because he would say it would be hard to shift a full-back but "if you have a goalscorer and he's not playing in your team, everyone is always on the look-out for a goalscorer so you'll always shift a player who is a goal threat".

That was what Forest had in that campaign and while we were always likely to score we were just as likely to be over-generous at the other end. For most of the first half of that season we floated around mid-table but after the turn of the year we began to climb the table. Our first game of 1984 saw us win 3-2 at Luton and in a run of seven unbeaten games we picked up 17 points before defeat at Arsenal saw us drop from second to third. We stayed third to the end of April when a goalless draw at Stoke dropped Forest to fifth. But we bounced back to end strongly, with three consecutive wins including a very satisfying 2-0 home win on the last day of the season over Manchester United, who had been vying with us for third place, and completed a league double over them with goals from two players with contrasting Old Trafford connections: Garry Birtles, who would probably rather forget his time at United and Viv Anderson, who would only enhance his

A star in the making

Heading for academia?

Spot the future European Cup winners: Kenny Swain – extreme right back row
Dennis Mortimer – extreme left front row, Terry McDermott – middle of front row

We were a close bunch
at Chelsea © *Getty Images*

Kenny Swain and Peter Withe act as bodyguards for Ron Saunders and the Football
League championship trophy © *Getty Images*

A rare outing for Kenny Swain
as Villa captain

Villa line up before the 1982 European Cup Final v Bayern Munich © *Getty Images*

Villa players, WAGs and the Football League championship trophy

Kenny Swain and the European Cup © *Getty Images*

Proud dad and footballer, Kenny with sons Stephen and Iain, and the European Cup

Pompey pin-up

Kenny Swain skippering Pompey to promotion v Crystal Palace

Kenny Swain celebrates Pompey promotion with his boyhood hero, manager Alan Ball

Kenny Swain in promotion-pushing action © *Getty Images*

Left: Kenny Swain, Crewe's oldest ever first team player. Right: Kenny Swain Crewe Alexandra coach (both images courtesy of Crewe Alexandra Football Club)

In conversation with the boss
© *Action Images*

National pride from one and all
© *Action Images*

Relief © *Action Images*

Tension © *Action Images*

Team England effort © *Action Images*

The job's a good 'un © *Action Images*

glittering career after he became Alex Ferguson's first signing. If United had beaten us they would have been in with a chance of pinching the runners-up spot from Southampton.

Although we lacked consistency in the league progress in Europe was a glamorous compensation. After eliminating Celtic we drew Sturm Graz. The first leg at home finished 1-0, with Paul Hart's late goal. When we went to Austria for the second leg they went 1-0 up from a 44th-minute penalty to level the aggregate score. Neither side could break the deadlock so we went into extra time where a Colin Walsh spot kick, six minutes from the end of extra time, sent us through to what would prove one of the most controversial European ties of all time. But only after a little bit of bother at the final whistle in which beer bottles flew in the general direction of anyone sporting Nottingham Forest colours. However there was another bit of controversy already brewing within the Forest ranks, and it was down to the very success we were having in the Uefa Cup and it came to a head just before we played the Austrian club.

While we were poor domestically we were in the last eight of the second most prestigious European club competition but there was no bonus provision in any of our contracts and it's fair to say some of the lads were getting a bit tetchy. The obvious course of action, to us anyway, was to approach Ian Bowyer and ask him what he was going to do about it, like he had any clue how to broach the subject with Cloughie. Before we played Graz we had a trip to Molineux but the day before that game the gaffer caught us, cold, on the Friday, having become aware of the unrest in the ranks. We had talked among ourselves on every aspect of our gripe from how much we should be asking for to who was actually going to do the asking.

Moving on to the front foot, which was how Cloughie always seemed to tackle problems, he motioned towards Ian Bowyer, as if he knew Bomber was favourite to bring up the subject with him. "Eh, captain, you lot are griping on about bonuses but what was the most important thing that this club has ever achieved, tell them captain." "Promotion to the First Division," Ian replied. "Exactly. You can stick your European Cups and your FA Cups and all the rest of it. The biggest achievement this club ever had was getting out of that Second Division into the First Division, never ever forget that. Without doing that we would never have had all the rest which is just icing on the cake. Bread and butter is what matters so when you're talking about bonuses and all the rest remember it's the f****** bread and butter that matters. Whatever happens with bonuses nothing gets agreed until we get a point at Wolves tomorrow, which reminds me, Kenneth, Hans, captain, you stay behind. The rest can go."

So as the others disappeared the three of us were looking rather sheepishly at each other because although we had been banging on among ourselves on the subject of bonuses we hadn't actually discussed specifics. The four of us stood there and Brian, straight to the point, said: "Go on then, I've heard you lot chuntering on, so what's your gripe?" Bomber spoke up first, saying: "Well, the fact is we haven't got anything in our contracts for European bonuses and we just feel that with a European final coming up we haven't had a penny so far." "True," said Brian, "I hear you."

"Well I think we should have something in there. "Not unreasonable, so what are you suggesting, how much are you after?" inquired Cloughie. Hans, who was not slow in coming forward, and a bit bolder and brasher than any of us, spoke up. "Well boss, I seenk it is reasonable to, maybe, suggest, mmm, £10,000." Brian mulled over the suggested figure, stroking his chin with thumb and forefinger, before replying: "Ten thousand between 18 players. I work that out at..." And before he could finish Hans, who was a big man, broke out in a kind of Jolly Green Giant laugh. "Yes, yes, ho, ho, ho, ho, yes." To which Cloughie responded: "Oh, you mean ten thousand each?" "I seenk so," said Hans. "You think that's reasonable, do you?" replied the manager. "I think it's reasonable," said the Dutch keeper, thinking we were making headway. "Tax-free of course?" added Brian. "Of course."

Brian continued: "£10,000, tax-free for 18, that's £180,000 tax-free, f****** 'ell you're a braver man than I Gunga Din. If you can find that tax-free, good luck to you. I hear what you're saying but you're in dreamland. However, I am not going to discuss it now but I reiterate what I said before about bread and butter. We come away with something from Wolves tomorrow and we'll talk again on Monday."

We relayed the message back to the rest of the players when we went for our usual Friday lunch of sausage and egg butties at the café just around the corner from the City Ground. We would usually be sitting there for a couple of hours and if it was your round you would be buying more than a dozen fried egg sandwiches, plus seconds which was often the case, plus chips, a real healthy diet, not. It was a social gathering that was so nice and unlike anything I had ever encountered at Chelsea or Villa and then we dispersed after letting everyone know we would be talking bonuses on Monday.

The game at Wolves was hard work and we were managing to hang in at 0-0 and looking for the "something" that Cloughie had demanded. Then Sod's Law. Wolves had a tricky right-winger, Danny Crainie, and he'd been having a good time against me and as we neared full-time he turned me inside out on the flank and raced towards the line. I tried to block him but he managed to chip a cross to the far post. I was flat on the ground but turned my head to see a ruck of players climb towards the ball, which ended up in the back of our net, via the head of Paul Hart.

"B*****s" I thought, "unbelievable". There was no time to recover and the final whistle went almost as soon as we restarted.

The hang-dog Forest players trudged off the Molineux pitch that afternoon into a dressing room where the only voice was ever going to be that of the manager and right on cue he let rip. "And you have the f***** audacity to talk to me about European bonuses. I tell you what, everything I said yesterday I f***** rescind. I rescind every single word I said yesterday about European bonuses because you can go and get stuffed." Naturally, there was never another word uttered about bonuses and we just got on with the job of pushing on in Europe. Next up, Anderlecht.

The first leg at home could not have gone better. We played very well and Steve Hodge scored both goals to put us in a very good position for the return. As we made our way over to Brussels it was in the forefront of my mind that it had been barely a couple of years since Villa's European Cup win which I thought was the pinnacle of my career and a time when I thought that career was nearly over. And there I was on the brink of another European final. I couldn't believe fate had been so kind.

Anderlecht were a good side, no doubt about that, which made our first leg victory all the more commendable. They had some very good players, most notably Enzo Scifo who played in four World Cups for Belgium. He was only about 19 then but already an established star so we knew we were in for a tough night but how tough we had no idea.

Where I was getting changed was directly opposite the corridor which led to the Anderlecht changing area, offices and rather curiously the referee's room. Cloughie was seated next to me and he'd spotted that suspicious proximity. "Eh Kenneth leave that f***** door open, wedge it if you have to. I want to see what's going on down there." He had obviously smelled a rat even then although no one had mentioned anything but he was agitated and a little bit stressed that evening. He called the club secretary Ken Smales over and asked: "Ken, those two who have just gone in that room just there, who are they? Go and find out." Ken went down the corridor, knocked on the door and after a short time he reported back to Brian that the two men he had seen entering the referee's room were Uefa officials. "Well, I just want you to keep an eye on them. What are they doing in the ref's room anyway?" However much Ken tried to convince him nothing was untoward Cloughie was ill at ease all evening and when the game kicked off we could see his concerns were justified because right from the off the referee's decisions were bizarre and we were grateful that Hans was in such great form despite his handicap. He was only playing because he had a pain-killing injection in his badly injured right hand and in front of him Paul Hart and Chris Fairclough were outstanding. Never the less Scifo pulled a goal back in the first half but we got to the interval still 2-1 to the good.

The gaffer continued to have his doubts about events on and off the field and wasn't afraid to voice those concerns. Indeed we even thought he wasn't going to let us go out for the second half. Although I never heard him say it I've been told that when the officials asked, for the third time, for us to make our way out for the second period Cloughie mockingly said, allegedly, "Oh I'm sorry did you want us?"

Just past the hour the conspiracy theorists took more notes as Kenneth Brylle made a fast run, with the ball, into the area. As he ran past me he clipped his own heel and fell over. I never touched him but he dived, convinced the referee I had and a penalty was awarded. He converted the spot-kick and that further galvanised our determination to take the game into extra time but two minutes from full-time van den Burgh fired past Hans to make it 3-2. Even then we kept going and with seconds remaining Paul Hart headed home what we thought was the deciding goal. As we wheeled around in triumph even the Anderlecht players had their heads bowed in resignation but amazingly, and without any reason, justification or explanation, the referee ruled out the goal and moments later blew the final whistle.

We just fell to our knees in disbelief. There were tears everywhere because, although they were a good side, we had switched off at the end and been caught out. But we took it on the chin and made our way back home, so near yet so far from a final we could have reached. It was only years later we found out that we SHOULD have reached it as details began to emerge that what Cloughie and most of us had suspected at the time, was in fact true. There was something amiss and the referee had been bribed. In September 1997 the then Anderlecht chairman admitted that his father paid £27,000 to the referee, Emilio Carlos Guruceta-Muro.

Apparently the referee had suffered a car accident in 1978 and, ironically, that was how he died nine years later. And details of the corruption that robbed us of a Uefa Cup Final only came to light when police were told that a Belgian gangster, who had acted as a middleman to transfer the money from the Anderlecht chairman to Senor Muro, had recorded the transaction allegedly for the sole purpose of blackmailing the club chairman, Constant Vanden Stock. In fact when his son admitted to his father's actions he confessed that it was common practice in those days to bribe officials.

By the time the suspicions became fact we players were already long retired but we felt we could not let it rest and decided to pursue legal action for missing out on a European final. We sought recompense to the tune of around 400,000 euros each and Nottingham Forest made its own claim seeking, compensation of 3.6 million euros. The players, I think there were 15 of us, each had to fill in a solicitor's questionnaire which included the following questions, with my answers.

Q. Where were you when the alleged contact occurred?
A. Just inside the penalty area.
Q. Did you observe the reaction of the linesman?
A. No.
Q. Did you say anything to the referee?
A. Yes I complained that I didn't trip him and that the Anderlecht forward had dived.
Q. Where were you when Paul Hart scored?
A. I was defending on the halfway line.

The questionnaire was used as the basis for a joint statement, which we all signed, in support of our claim. Years of judicial squabbling followed before the case was eventually dropped as recently as 2007. Our case was not driven by money. No amount of cash would have compensated for the lost opportunity of playing in a European final.

Nowadays when I address our England youngsters about doping and doping control I inform them of the protocol they must be prepared for after each game and not just after games, it could be after training. It is a necessary measure to combat cheating and seeking to gain an unfair advantage. I try to make them understand the reasons why all that is taking place is to protect them and I explain that until they have suffered at the hands of such underhand tactics, as Forest did against Anderlecht, it is hard to imagine what it feels like.

In the World Cup in Mexico, in 2011, I asked our Under-17s to imagine how they would feel if they lost and were eliminated and it turned out that the guy who had scored the winner had been taking performance-enhancing drugs. Drugs that have helped him speed past "you, and you and you who have been working all your lives, sleeping properly and eating properly etc etc. How would you feel? Absolutely devastated and rightly so".

Even though, in my heart of hearts, I felt Anderlecht were the better side than us on the night there was too much wrong, most notably the penalty decision and our disallowed goal. Then to find out all those years later that there was substance in the suspicions we harboured back then and confessions were coming out. There was no compensation for us. That was our opportunity, our livelihood affected. Someone had taken that from us, robbed us of our chance. And even if we had been successful in the courts and secured financial recompense, so what? You don't want that, you just wanted the opportunity which we never had because of underhand behaviour.

After the defeat in Brussels it was very tense inside the Forest camp and that manifested itself as we were going up the steps to board the flight home. Brian, who was stressed out like I had never witnessed before, was in a hurry to get on with the homeward journey and was pushing and shoving his way up the steps. My wife, who was fearful of flying at the best of times, was similarly in a hurry. Lily snapped at him and he muttered something back before we finally boarded and took our seats.

During the flight Brian came down the plane to where we were seated and proceeded to explain himself and apologise for his behaviour. It wasn't the most eloquent of apologies but when he mentioned he didn't like flying Lily admitted likewise and there was a mutuality of understanding that smoothed over the earlier clash. So he was human, he wasn't always right but it was a fallibility he was quick to acknowledge and he knew himself if he had been wrong. He didn't need anyone to point that out to him and when he was out of line he was quick to hold up his hands and admit it.

There was another occasion when Brian's fear of flying manifested into a drastic course of action. Forest would occasionally jet out to play in remote, far flung places and there was an incident that made the headlines one time when we were on our way to Abu Dhabi.

We played Arsenal on the Saturday, (25th February 1984) and were drawing 0-0, until Paul Mariner broke through in the last minute to snatch the winner. We were naturally deflated when we met up early the following morning for the coach trip down to Heathrow and our flight. We weren't really relishing something most of us regarded as a Middle East jaunt of three or four days' pain for which there was no gain. Of course we knew the club were getting a fee for the trip and Cloughie's take was always "we have to fund our existence by taking on these little trips" so it was a case of grin and bear it.

As we got to the airport the boss was still seething that we lost the day before. We had to board an aircraft that was on its way to Bombay, that was just the way it had been organised and the first stop was our destination. Cloughie just kept moaning and as we sat on the plane he directed his displeasure towards the guy who had organised the travel plans, complaining: "He's sat up there in the posh seats at the front, drinking champagne while we, the reason for this trip, are consigned to cattle class." It wasn't quite that bad but there were loads of screaming kids in our sitting area and it just so happened that one particularly loud infant was just in front of Brian propped up on a parent's shoulder and giving the full vocal delivery right into Cloughie's face.

"That is all I need. We've been beaten 1-0, you've got him sitting up the front and we've got to sit in these delightful conditions for seven f***** hours." So he leaned over and said to Bomber: "If we get back from this I'm telling you now you can have every penny we make out of this trip, I swear to you. You can have the f***** lot because this is too much."

It got worse. The plane taxied into position and as we built up speed it bounced up and down on the runway, babies still screaming, then suddenly BANG! The brakes locked on and bags flew all over the cabin, cups, belongings, everything and everyone is s******g themselves as the plane slid off the main runway. The intercom clicked and we heard the announcement: "Sorry, ladies and gentlemen, but there has been a technical hitch and we have to return to the terminal. We're hoping it won't take too long to sort out but we are going to disembark all passengers."

That was it. Cloughie, who had been close to breaking point anyway, was tipped over the edge. "That's it. We're off." He turned to Ronnie Fenton and instructed him to tell the purser. We sat there quietly, not knowing what was going to happen next but damned sure something would. Fifteen minutes or so later the purser made his way down the plane in the direction of the Forest party, saying "good morning" right and left as he passed the passengers. Their faces showed shock and relief, in equal measure, that they weren't a blazing mass of tangled metal featured on the evening news. Then he reached us. "Good morning Mr Clough, what can we do for you?" "I tell you what you can do for us. We'd like to get off the plane. We're getting off," said Brian. "It's not that easy Mr Clough, we can't do that."

Cloughie, not allowing the purser to speak, retorted: "Well we got on without a problem so I don't see any problems getting off." Then the purser tried to get officious, bad move! "Well you've already been through passport control…" "So we'll go back through passport control because I've got me passport with me now," added Brian, reasonably. "Ah, but there's all sorts of other things, like security…" By this time Cloughie had gone into hyper logical mode. "Look, we walked on without a problem. We've paid for our tickets. You've had our money, I've got me passport and we travel light at Nottingham Forest so we've got our bags with us so we're getting off when they bring the steps."

The purser disappeared and shortly afterwards the steps arrived at the aircraft and the doors were opened. The gaffer shot off so we grabbed our bags and followed him to the exit as Brian politely shoved his way past other passengers, "excuse me, sorry love" etc. At the door the stewardess tried to stop us but our leader swept past her and we all followed dutifully.

We got back to the terminal and caught them by surprise because they had seen us board the aircraft and didn't expect anyone to emerge from behind them so they were facing the wrong way. But we were approached by a chap in a British Airways uniform who bellowed out "hold on, you can't do this". Brian repeated his earlier declaration that we had paid our money and walked on with no problem so that entitled us to walk off, adding: "We've had to walk off and now we want to go home, thank you very much." And that's exactly what we did and when I got home that afternoon my wife was a little surprised to see me four days early minus a tan. Naturally it made the news how, orchestrated by Brian Clough, the Forest team had marched back through customs and passport control almost as soon as they had marched through.

Brian Clough was a one-off. Before my time he was a one-off as a player and as a manager he was probably THE one-off. There has never been a manager like him and I doubt there ever will. It was a privilege to play for him, despite initial reservations, and I have only been able to give the merest insight into him, even after spending two-and-a-half years at Nottingham Forest.

To many his style of management was spontaneous, impulsive, but I soon learnt it was nothing of the sort. He told me he never picked his team without consulting his backroom staff of Alan Hill and Liam O'Kane, and his number two, Ronnie Fenton. Each of them had their own role and each made a contribution, they weren't ornaments. As a manager Brian had a unique approach to tactics. He didn't really have to be a tactician, he would leave that to his players. Tactics revolved around the state and the belief of his players, he never spoke about the opposition. Whereas Bill Shankly's approach was psychological, as demonstrated by his legendary 'appraisal' of Bobby Moore as being unable to "run, head or tackle", Cloughie wasn't like that. He was always respectful but on the day of a game he wouldn't demonstrate too much respect for the opposing players; indeed he would almost suggest that we weren't really good enough and shouldn't even be there that day and it was that reverse psychology that was the motivation for us to prove him wrong, which we invariably did. Equally he could be totally ambivalent at the quality of the opposition.

I remember one trip to Old Trafford and although United were a big club they were nothing like the monster club they are now. And when we arrived Brian bowled through the place and any sort of portrayal of prestige he encountered, by staff or symbol, he would be contemptuous of and it was genuine contempt. He would always acknowledge humility but was quite the opposite of anything or anyone pretentious and that was why he was so good at man-management, he was so down to earth. Anyone with delusions of grandeur got short shrift from Brian Clough and he never had any players like that for long, because he wouldn't tolerate them. It would be too simplistic to say that was his secret but he did make some star players and bought a few also as well as making top players out of some, like myself, who were considered more as sow's ears than what Cloughie made us. But that's what he could do, he could make a player realise his potential and a significant part of that was down to the self-esteem he generated from someone and the value he placed on their contribution. In effect by, perhaps, understating our right to be there he gave us the incentive to move up to that level of expectation which most of his players did, because of him. And they would do it week in, week out because of the general atmosphere Brian would generate.

Brian Clough rarely made a mistake when assessing a player's ability. Even rarer were his misjudgements as far as character was concerned. He had no truck with Big-time Charlies and was quick to act if anyone began to get ahead of themselves after they arrived. And if they would not conform to his ways they were quickly shipped out. He ran a ship that was basically happy as exemplified by the family and social aspect of certain away trips.

He also had a special take on captaincy. I was proud to captain Villa on the rare occasions Denis Mortimer didn't play but Brian Clough had very different views on captaincy. He never appeared to like anything to do with status, never seemed to accord any esteem, treating his captain like any other member of the team, nothing special. It wasn't intentional; that's just the way Cloughie was. His advice to the skipper before a game, any game, used to be "win the toss", and that was it.

Cloughie used to say: "It's not easy, management. Making the right decisions at any time is difficult. The best managers get more decisions right than wrong and that's always the sign of a good manager when you get more right than wrong."

If there is such a thing as a natural manager Brian Clough was one. I never knew the likes of Matt Busby or Bill Shankly but I guess they would come into the same category. However, those managers were a completely different breed to what football has these days. As people are a product of their generation, their environment, so too are managers and their values were either because of their upbringing or despite it. I think most people who are knowledgeable about football are aware of Brian Clough growing up in the austerity of the post-war North East, and the legendary status he earned scoring goals for Middlesbrough and Sunderland at very nearly a goal a game. He always loved going back to that area and there was an episode during one trip when we were to play Sunderland, at Roker Park, in a midweek fixture, which illustrated him perfectly.

Brian was a fiercely loyal person, giving and expecting loyalty in equal proportions and the Sunday prior to that game there was a pretty disparaging newspaper exposé, by John McGovern on Kenny Burns. Cloughie was very upset and it must have stewed on his mind for days because, half an hour before kick-off, he addressed the players as we were getting changed. It wasn't a formal team edict, just a general discourse, having a go at the article and its writer. He said: "Did you read all that bloody rubbish on Sunday. I can't believe it, the way McGovern laid into Burnsie and his alcoholic ways and how we had to carry him up the stairs he was that p****d and all the rest of it, bloody awful things to say. I don't remember reading in the article about the night Kenny Burns carried the whole lot of us in Cologne. He carried the whole f***** team, sober or not, that night so McGovern can go and get lost. He's not welcome at our ground anymore."

I don't know how things finished up with John McGovern or where it went thereafter but it was striking how Brian was upset by a perceived lack of loyalty by one former player, historically one of his top men, having a go at another. It certainly impacted on our dressing room that night and no matter what Kenny's reputation was Brian stuck by him. It was a loyalty born out of players doing what he expected of them and more. He made good players out of poor players and great players out of good ones. He is legendary for making many a silk purse out of many a sow's ear, I should know.

I also remember that Brian Clough could also be very uncomplimentary towards his players. John Robertson is synonymous with Cloughie more than most yet the gaffer would still comment on Robbo's shabby look and his smoking habit. But he did rate the player. I remember before one game Brian asked me: "Kenneth, how far can you kick it?" Confused, I began looking around, pleading silently for help. He repeated the question and when no help was forthcoming from the rest of the lads I decided to go for it. "What do you mean boss?" "I mean, if you took a goal-kick, Kenneth, where would the ball land? Would it land on the centre circle, would it land beyond there, would it even reach the centre-circle? How far can you kick it?" "It would probably drop 20, 25 yards in their half, about 70 yards," I said. "Well, kick it f***** 80 and if you can't kick it 80 give it to the little fat fellah in front of you because he can look after the ball. So, if you've got a problem either kick it 80 yards or give it to him."

He also welcomed back former players with great warmth whenever they dropped in, which was often. John O'Hare, for example, came in one day and word reached Brian who made sure John was treated with great affection. "Come in John, lovely to see you," he said as he gave him a big hug and a kiss before sitting him down. Then, as he was prone to do, he turned to one of the Forest forwards who was nearby and pontificated: "Hey, you, call yourself a striker. Now this man here, he was a striker. He could score goals. You think you can score goals well let me tell you this fellah COULD score goals." Brian was brilliant like that with players. He could make them feel ten feet tall.

Perhaps the most talked about player under Brian Clough at Forest was his son Nigel. There was no question about his playing ability because there was little doubt, from an early age, he was going to be a player, which he justified by going on to play for England. The general interest was more the situation of a son being a player under his father.

Nigel started to emerge as I went into my final year at Forest. Brian had often mentioned going to see him play in a junior game or similar and how he preferred that to doing just about anything else, including managing Forest as I recall. So we, the players, knew Nigel could play and it was no surprise when he joined the club. He more than held his own as a player but most of the interest beyond the club seemed to centre on how their relationship, literally, impacted on how Brian dealt with Nigel as a player.

The truth is that Nigel always got short shrift from his dad, there were never any favours, expected or granted. Indeed I felt Brian was, on occasion, a touch, unnecessarily harsh, as if to reinforce there would be no favouritism. But generally they just avoided each other and Nigel toed the line anyway. As far as the other players were concerned we treated him like any other player and although he wasn't in the first team we respected him as a person and as a fellow professional. He was a bloody good player, quite a strong lad, and he could retain possession of the ball. As he developed, in later years, people would question his lack of pace but technically he was very good with instant control of the ball being his forte. He was very good with his back to goal and of course he was an excellent finisher so he obviously inherited some of his father's traits, according to my father who had seen Clough in his prime and, of course, according to Brian himself.

Though fiercely loyal Brian Clough could also be very damning and unlike his general demeanour, which was polarised between black and white, he could occasionally hit somewhere in between. I remember we were preparing for an away game having come off the back of a 1-0 defeat that was down to a naive mistake from a young player's decision to play a square ball when a square ball was not on, in our own half. It was a safety and risk scenario where an individual has to weigh up both and come to an appropriate decision. As a coach I have become more aware just how big an element of safety and risk there is in football. But that youngster's poor decision proved costly as his pass was intercepted and in a matter of seconds the ball was in the back of our net and Cloughie was furious. He slaughtered young Colin Walsh as a consequence, stating the obvious that he "had cost us three points". When he finished his tirade he then threw in his bit of carrot after such copious amounts of stick.

"But you can redeem yourself next week son because you're the first on the team sheet. No one else is at this point but you are and being on the team sheet next week I would like you to bring your mum and dad down, and the family, at our club's expense. Tell them to come down on the Friday night. We'll put them up in the Holiday Inn because I want them to come and see their son play for Nottingham Forest at the City Ground, so will you do that?"

Colin had obviously been sick as the proverbial parrot but within seconds of knocking him down Cloughie had picked him back up and he was brilliant like that. But he could be just as contrary and knock someone back down to earth with a healthy dose of reality.

Early in my time at the club, I had only been there a week, we were due to play at West Brom. I asked what time we were to meet up for the coach and Brian told me there was no need for me to travel over, "you only live down the road, just meet us at the ground". So I turned up around 6.30pm and met up with the team just after they arrived and I walked in as he was talking to the players. "Eh up Kenneth, come in. We were just talking about that nightclub in Nottingham, what's it called Chris (Fairclough), that one you go to?" An embarrassed Chris denied any knowledge and said, sheepishly: "I don't go there." Brian continued: "Come on, Fashanu (Justin) said to me, 'just because I go to a gays' club doesn't mean I am gay…' Well, I thought, blow me, I'm not having that. Listen, if I want to go and see a movie I go to a cinema. If I want to pray I go to church so don't tell me you're going to a gay club and you're not gay."

I think the most unique thing about Brian Clough was his unpredictability but almost as soon as I pulled on a Forest shirt I quickly learnt that was the beauty of working under him. It was the expectation, the understanding, of knowing every day something was going to happen because he was there every day and you were going to come into contact with him at some point during the day. It was a breath of fresh air to me at that stage in my life and career. It was a little strange because I wasn't a young player but he did have an effect on people. He made people feel better about themselves, and filled them with self-esteem and confidence.

He had this gift of being able to instil self-esteem if it wasn't there in the first place but he could also nurture it if it already existed. He was very good at rekindling that characteristic if it had been lost. He really valued everyone – not just his players but his backroom staff and everyone who worked at his football club. In fact his secretary at Nottingham Forest, Carol, who was at the club for a very long time, years later told me a story that illustrated just how kind he was.

She had a friend who was in a similar position at Huddersfield Town who told her of the time they were exchanging stories about what their respective managers had bought them for Christmas. Carol's friend told her that the Town manager had bought her a brand new washing machine and when she asked Carol what Brian had bought her for Christmas she revealed that Brian had stumped up for a brand new kitchen!

Brian had a reputation for being mercenary but all I ever saw was generosity. From stories I was told and some of the things I saw him do I can only judge as I saw and what I saw was not mercenary, it was selfless.

There was another story, and ironically it happened at another away fixture at Sunderland, maybe it was something about the air up there. There were two kids outside the Forest hotel in Seaham, where we used to stay, ten-year-old Craig and 11-year-old Aaron Bromfield. The brothers were collecting autographs and I signed their books and told them if they wanted the rest of the players they would have to return the next day. They turned up the following morning, at breakfast time, and I met them and brought them into the hotel lobby and got a few of the players to sign autographs. They were knocked out by that, really bright-eyed at the experience, a couple of nice, fresh-faced and well mannered North East kids who were obviously football daft.

Cloughie got wind of what was going on and turned up and happily stood there, chatting away to these two young fans who couldn't believe their luck that they were in the company of Brian Clough. Brian then invited them to have lunch with the team, with the caveat: "Go home and tell your mum and dad you're coming to have lunch with Nottingham Forest. Would you like to come to the game today?" Gobsmacked, they nodded their heads vigorously and managed to utter "yes" in between large intakes of breath. "Well tell your mum and dad we'll get you some tickets and we'll meet them at the ground, ok?"

So they went home and came back, suitably cleaned up, at lunchtime and those two urchins ended up seated at the end of our table enjoying a pre-match meal and every so often Brian referred to the brothers. But that wasn't all because when we had finished eating Cloughie urged them to jump on the team bus with us. When we got to Roker Park Brian brought them into the changing room before they disappeared into their complimentary seats for the game to complete a memorable day for a couple of football loving kids who only turned up to collect a few autographs and ended up with a memory for life. For many years later Brian and those two lads kept in touch and they were frequently invited down to spend the weekend with Brian and Barbara at their house and well into adulthood those two lads kept in touch with the family.

So Brian Clough could be fiercely loyal but he could be quite the opposite if anyone crossed him or, more to the point, crossed the line beyond his established parameters of behaviour. He used to say: "Bull****, I can smell it a mile off."

I only mention Peter Taylor, in passing, because he was no longer part of the famous double act with Brian by the time I played for him. But there is one story concerning Cloughie's former sidekick which demonstrates perfectly how he would respond when he felt betrayed.

It was the time when John Robertson was leaving Forest, shortly after I arrived at the club. Peter Taylor had only been gone a year and the story, as I heard it, was that Brian had worked so hard to get Peter a testimonial for his services to Nottingham Forest. He had to persuade the board that Peter was worth it but he managed it and so Peter received a healthy sum from that testimonial because it was his plan to retire and Brian wanted him to walk away with enough to ensure a comfortable retirement. But within six months Peter was back and not only that he was back as manager at Derby County just down the road, leaving Cloughie, who had fought tooth and nail to get him a testimonial, with egg on his face. But, to add insult to injury, it seems that Peter never informed Brian and he topped it off by signing John Robertson, who was out of contract at Forest, without any consultation with his close friend.

Brian only found out when he was on a charity walk somewhere up north so he wasn't best pleased and all those years of friendship and loyalty were brushed aside. Although some years later Brian did express regret at some of the things he came out with in the wake of what he perceived as a betrayal, he always regretted not making his peace with Peter, something Barbara later confirmed.

In preparation for season 1984/85 Cloughie arranged a trip to Holland for a pre-season friendly after a transfer spending spree when he spent big on three players. Johnny Metgod, who came from Real Madrid, was a strapping six foot two inches tall with a reputation as a goal-scoring midfielder but could play anywhere. Gary Megson joined us from Sheffield Wednesday and Trevor Christie, who had been banging in goals for fun just down the road at Notts County. Trevor had no trouble settling in because he was a local lad and most of the Forest lads knew him but Gary found it a bit hard to ease his way in to the fold. It wasn't helped by his regular habit of throwing up before a game. Ten minutes before kick-off while the rest of the lads would be talking or having a laugh he would have his head down a toilet bowl retching up full stomach contents with the mandatory heaving noises. Cloughie would turn around and in sheer disgust say: "Blow me, what on earth have I signed here. I can't put up with all this."

And he didn't, not for long anyway. I do know that in a short spell with Forest Gary never made a single first team appearance but he was always there on Friday mornings when the squad assembled in the boardroom at the City Ground, for a drink. On one particular occasion the gaffer sat next to Gary, intentionally. Brian began to talk about what we were going to do in the game the following day to the assembled players then he turned to Gary, tapped him on the knee and said: "Oh, and by the way, are you ever going to move to Nottingham or what? It's about f***** time you moved 'cos it is in your contract."

Gary was a bit shell-shocked at the way normally private business was opened up to public scrutiny but Cloughie was like that and prone to throw things out into the open. And in that particular instance it was almost a case of the manager throwing the gauntlet down to a player because it was obviously getting to Brian as well. Eventually after just four months with Forest Cloughie sold Gary to Newcastle United for less than he paid.

It always struck me that Gary in those days had a little more nous than he should have considering his age and his background, with his father Don being a Sheffield Wednesday legend. Certainly not fully subscribing to the ethos of the club was something that seemed to upset Cloughie. He was okay with us, his fellow players, but Gary obviously found it difficult to embrace the Nottingham Forest way, the Brian Clough way, and I think it was as simple as that. If you didn't take to Brian, or the club, that was it. Some years later Gary was doing some scouting for the Football Association having been quite successful as a manager, and we bumped into each other at a game and as we met the first thing he said to me was: "Don't talk to me about Forest. I don't want to be reminded I could never quite cut it with Cloughie." He basically admitted that the whole Nottingham Forest experience was beyond him and that he found it a very traumatic time.

Brian, post-Forest days, once told me of a similar case involving Asa Hartford who had been signed by him, from Manchester City, a few years earlier and it was another example of Mr Clough's modus operandi which was corroborated by Asa some years later.

Brian had told me the background to the events at the time about Asa, who only had a few months at Forest and a handful of games but never the less he did speak highly of Brian despite his move not working out. Asa told me that Cloughie had been "brilliant". But he went on to say: "Cloughie pulled me aside one day and told me he felt he had made a mistake in buying me, saying that I wasn't quite the player he thought I was. He went on to tell me he had misjudged me, saying he thought I couldn't actually do what he had expected of me." Asa said that Brian paid him all he was due in his contract, shook his hand and that was it, he was gone. It was the same with Justin Fashanu although it appeared that was more a Peter Taylor signing than Brian's. Never the less Forest made him the first £1m black footballer when he signed from Norwich as a 19-year-old and that was just a year after Brian made Trevor Francis the first £1m player. Ironically, Justin joined as a replacement for Trevor after he joined Manchester City.

But Cloughie quickly decided Justin wasn't worth the outlay, and quickly shipped him down the road to Notts County for a fraction of what he paid for him, after a loan spell at Southampton. It was a costly mistake but proved he acted quickly when he recognised his errors.

That was how Brian worked. He rarely made a mistake with a player, but once he recognised his misjudgement he acted quickly and put it behind him. But, now the background is in place about those new players Cloughie brought in, the story of Johnny Metgod and our game in Rotterdam.

Pre-season friendlies have always been a part of easing new players into a team set-up but at Forest there were the extra demands of Brian's way of playing. We went to Holland and it was a particularly hot summer and the pitches were rock hard. With Cloughie it didn't matter if you were playing a friendly, a testimonial, a league game or a cup game, he demanded a performance and total commitment. And there was one particular game in which we were struggling to stay in contention and found ourselves 2-0 down, and it could have been more. The temperature must have been knocking 90 degrees and we were grateful to make it to half-time at least as respite from the heat. But in the dressing room you could have cut the atmosphere with a knife.

Pre-season friendly or not we were losing. Brian Clough was losing. Silence reigned and we sat there unable to pick our heads up. No one wanted to make eye contact so we sat, as one, with our elbows on our knees. The best we could do was to circle our eyes to see where the gaffer was walking. If he was in one area you could risk a quick look up to see people's reactions in another area. That lasted for what seemed an unearthly amount of time but was at least four minutes. We knew it was going to end but no one knew when. Then Cloughie spoke. "Go on Ron, I'll have another one." So Ronnie Fenton poured him a drink and he sat there swirling it around in his plastic cup. It was the only sound in the deathly silence. Then Brian started laughing. At first just a couple of bursts of light laughter, then it got progressively louder. He stood up and laughed again. It was just like a nightmare, a horror movie, because we knew what was coming. Then the moment came, he spoke.

"Hey lads, what a f****** good judge I am." By this time we were looking at him because he had made the first eye contact so it was all right to look back. "What a f****** good judge I am." And he walked over to Johnny Metgod, looked at him, eyeball to eyeball, and pointed his finger at Johnny and delivered his damning verdict. "I paid £500,000 for a six-foot-two midfield player who can't f****** head it." Then he walked over to the other side of the room and addressed Trevor Christie. "I paid £350,000 for a striker who couldn't hit a f****** barn door." Then it was Gary Megson's turn and the now famous quote: "And I paid £250,000 for a midfield player who couldn't trap a f****** bag of cement." He turned to Ronnie Fenton and repeated his previous self-assessment. "What a f****** good judge I am Ron." Meanwhile I was sat there thinking, "don't look at me, please don't look at me" because if he did I was all set to shout back "what do you want for a free transfer?" But Brian still hadn't finished. He turned to Ronnie Fenton and added: "Do you know what Ron, if I was chairman of this football club I would sack me now having paid over £1 million of this club's hard-earned money on these three."

Although Gary moved on Johnny and Trevor soon settled into the team although it was Peter Davenport who was making the headlines with five goals in the first three league games of 1984/85, including a hat-trick against Sunderland, the first First Division hat-trick of the season. Johnny got his first goal when we beat Arsenal and then we went to Villa Park and won 5-0 for Forest's biggest ever win at Villa. Trevor scored his first goals, three of them. A 3-1 win over Luton, all the goals coming in a 14-minute spell, took Forest to the top of the table in mid-September, but from then on it was downhill and we never got back higher than second.

We did have the briefest of diversions with another, much shorter, Uefa Cup adventure. Whoever handled the draw in Zurich must have had a weird sense of humour because we were handed a tie against another Belgian side, Bruges, just five months after the Anderlecht fiasco and the symmetry wasn't going to end there. After beating Luton we played the first leg at home and drew 0-0 which wasn't the best of results to take to Belgium. It was to be a forgettable trip for me, personally and professionally.

We flew out on the Monday afternoon and just chilled out. The following day, because the hotel had a leisure complex, some of us went for a swim and as I pushed away from the side of the pool I felt a sharp pain in my foot. I hopped out of the water and looked down to see a pool of blood issuing forth from my right foot, across the marble tiles. Looking at a gash down the middle of my foot my first thought was "what's he (Cloughie) going to say?" My second thought was "s**t, that's me out of the game".

It needed stitches and my main concern was keeping it secret because I still wanted to play. Bomber and a couple of others had seen what happened but I had a problem because stitches were needed and if I went to see the physio that would be curtains for my involvement against Bruges. So I went to reception and asked where I could see a doctor. He sorted me out with three stitches and a jab and it only cost me £30 so I thought I was safe. Unfortunately I woke the next morning and the pain was killing me. I took some anti-inflammatory tablets and after a sleep that afternoon I was sure I was going to be okay, especially swathed in bandages. But the pain wasn't long in coming back so I knew I was just digging a deeper hole. I'd injured myself, not reported it, had it stitched unofficially and there I was on match day about to declare I wasn't going to be fit. But after an afternoon kip the pain began to subside so my Great Escape was back on and I decided to keep schtum and hope for the best.

But I worried how I was going to hide all the padding that made my right shoe look like a size 11. I decided I would go to the changing room in trainers, disappear into the toilet taking my match socks with me and wrap the bandages around my injury and hope the size differential between my right and left feet wasn't too obvious. I trotted out with the rest of the lads and somehow managed to get through the game all right ,mainly down to a polishing of the skill of kicking a ball with the outside of the foot, EVERY TIME. But my discomfort was compounded by Willy Wellens' winning goal in the last minute and we were out.

A week later we were due to go to Malta, another of Cloughie's away breaks, so with about ten days between games I thought I was home and dry. But lazing by the pool in Malta, flip flops dangling, Ronnie Fenton walked past and spotted the gash. Naturally he inquired so I had to be creative in telling him I had forked myself in the garden. "That needs stitches, that." I smiled and nodded, "ok with steristrips", result.

That was to prove my last season as a Forest player and we struggled for consistency all the way through the campaign. As early as September we were top of the table and Peter Davenport topped the scoring charts but that was as good as it got. We did get to fourth by February on the back of a run of six wins in a seven-game spell but the club then took on another of their flights of fancy with a five-day trip to war-torn Iraq.

Before our first game against the Iraqi national team we were presented to Saddam Hussein and I think we were all grateful that we were only visiting. However, there were strong rumours at the time that it may not have been the Iraqi leader. He is alleged to have used a number of "doubles" in case of assassination attempts. If Saddam wasn't there he wasn't the only one. Brian Clough, as he was prone to do, decided he would be better off elsewhere. It wasn't the only thing he missed as the month before he went to Tenerife and missed out on the award he was going to be presented with by the Midland Football Writers to mark his tenth anniversary as Forest manager.

We drew 1-1 against the Iraq national team and lost the second game but it was less than comforting that we could hear shelling from the hotel where we slept albeit in the distance. Fortunately we only slept at the hotel and spent most of our time at the British Embassy. A few weeks later the hotel was bombed!

Safely back home we won at Southampton but started to slide down the table and finished ninth. So it was the end of my stint as a Forest player but Brian still had one or two surprises in store. The biggest one was inviting me over to his house for a meal.

I knew that departing Forest I was leaving behind perhaps the most enigmatic and, arguably, the best manager in the land, his words not mine, though I would not argue. But, as you might expect the unexpected where Brian Clough was concerned I was not disappointed. Surprised but not disappointed. When all the paperwork was done, after

117

asking me if everything had gone through okay, he whispered: "You know you can still stay, for another year, if you want." I thanked him for being so kind but admitted that I might struggle to get in the team so it was time to move on. "You're a good judge but I would still have no problem if you wanted to stay."

When Lily and I travelled over to Brian's house for lunch he threw us another curve ball and told us we were eating at Kedleston Hall. He then invited us back to his house for a farewell drink.

We sat there on a lovely sunny afternoon, watching the cricket of course because he loved his cricket. He changed out of his suit into his renowned green tracksuit top and shorts and put his feet up. He turned to his wife and asked, "Barbara, will you get me and Kenneth a drink please?" She brought us two glasses of champagne and Lily disappeared into the kitchen with her leaving me and Brian, watching the match, chatting about the previous two-and-a-half years at Forest and putting the football world to rights.

He was a great conversationalist and in the comfort of his own home was very open as we spoke. He asked me where I saw my future after I stopped playing and I told him I wanted to go into coaching or management. Then he dropped his guard somewhat and came out with a bit of a bombshell. He said: "Don't make the mistakes I've made, like when I went into Leeds United. I made a big mistake and I regret it. It was the right club to go to and the right time but I went about it in the wrong way. I was a bit young and a bit brash in those days and I know I upset too many people. I probably wouldn't do that again given the same circumstances. I did have a few gripes with Leeds but, having said that, they were good to me. They did enable me to pay off my house, lock, stock and barrel and I did come away with a new Mercedes, so it wasn't all bad news. So what I am saying to you Kenneth, is this. When you do go into a club, as manager or coach, don't rock the boat. Have a look at it first, assess it before you make any changes."

Then he changed tack again. He asked me if I had ever seen his study. I said "how could I, you've never even invited me to your house before". Quick as ever he said he only ever invited players over "when I sign them not when they're leaving".

I had gone prepared for that first visit which would also be my last. Because I knew Brian was a big Frank Sinatra fan, he was always belting out some classic or other, I decided to buy him a farewell gift, a superb boxed set of LPs, *The Capitol Years*. In fact I was so impressed with it, I bought one for myself.

So there we were in Cloughie's inner sanctum when he leaned over and picked up a framed picture which he handed to me. "What do you think of this then?" because he knew I was a Sinatra fan also. In the picture was Brian Clough and Francis Albert Sinatra, with their arms around each other's shoulder. If that wasn't enough to bowl me over, and it did, the sentiment written on it was: "To Old Big 'ead from Ol Blue Eyes". Priceless.

It was obviously an emotional time for me and I am not ashamed to admit that when Lily and I left Brian's house that day we were in tears. He'd given us a couple of bottles of champagne and boxes of chocolates, which was typical of the man and as we were getting in the car he shouted over. "Don't forget, when we play Southampton pop across and see us at the hotel, the usual place. Come over the night before and have dinner. Anyway, must dash because I've got to go and sign your replacement." I asked, "who?" "Young lad at Coventry City, Stuart Pearce." "A good player him, I like him," as if Brian Clough needed my endorsement. "So do I, and he can kick it with his left foot as well." He always had to have the last word, and he did that day.

After I left Forest I rarely bumped into Brian as our careers went in different directions but the impact on me and the memories of my time as a player under him are with me to this day and will always be part of me. As I commit my feelings and recollections about Brian Clough to print they bring with them mixed feelings of emotion, sadness and happiness, similar to what I experienced when I went to a memorial service in his honour, in 2004. It was due to be held in Derby Cathedral but it wasn't big enough for the 15,000 who were to attend so it was switched to Pride Park Stadium where Forest and Derby fans as well as many former players were united in their homage.

There was a paradox about how I felt that day when compared with the occasions when I revisited Aston Villa over the years. I actually felt a little out of place among the many players Brian turned into title winners. They were his champions and I felt I shouldn't be there. At Villa I would get a similar feeling that other people were uncomfortable when they were with the players who had won the league championship and European Cup. Having said that there were enough younger players there, like Viv Anderson, Bryn Gunn and Chris Fairclough who pulled me into the group because, alongside the likes of Kenny Burns and Larry Lloyd, I almost felt I was an "honorary" member of the Forest ensemble. I was privileged to be there paying my respects. I was privileged to play under Brian Clough. Indeed it was a privilege to experience him.

Brian was inspiring as a person and he inspired me. I'm not talking about motivation. I found him inspirational just with his outlook, his bravery and courage. He had utter conviction in his opinions and ways though with very little flexibility, none in fact. He was as black and white as it is possible to be. He could also reduce football to a meaningless level. I don't mean he made it unimportant but he could eliminate the pressure of a football situation to nothing and with that he took all the pressure away, for his players. At other times it could be the most important thing imaginable, the end of the world, if it hadn't gone well. He would say: "It's your livelihood young men, my livelihood… and you're not taking bread out of my kids' mouths." He had that ferocity about him. He had so much passion about him that there was nothing tedious about being part of his orbit. It was something to be enjoyed, something to be enthralled by.

Being at the memorial service and seeing Chris Fairclough again reminded me of the importance the gaffer used to place on playing for supporters and team-mates because of something he once said to Chris just ahead of kick-off one day. The boss swept in, sat down among us and looked over to where Chris was changing. "Blow me," he said. "You look like a rabbit in the headlights. You look frightened to death son. You'd better get that look off your face in the next 20 minutes because you're about to go on to a stage in front of 28,000 and every single one of them loves you and you're playing with some of the most talented players in the country who will fight tooth and nail for you. So don't walk out with a face like that whatever you do. This is a day to enjoy so no need to be looking like that." And it worked. It always did.

Brian Clough was very big on discipline, self-discipline and imposed. Whether it was professional or social discipline he demanded it, especially from his players, and he would not stand for any kind of back chat to referees. If anyone got booked for talking back to referees they suffered the consequences, financial and heavy. Cloughie was forever telling people to shut up and get on with the game. "I don't want to hear you complaining, I just want you to get on with the game and leave the referee to get on with his" was a regular mantra.

There was one incident involving Johnny Metgod, who was as vociferous at complaining on the park as Cloughie was off it but Johnny was opinionated to boot and Brian did not like that. He saw the game as a football job and as players our job was simple. "Your job is to head it and kick it if you're a defender and stick it in the back of the net if you're a forward. And if you're somewhere in the middle stop it going in your goal and try and create something in the other goal."

His rules were basic and unequivocal. On the few occasions I was on the touchline with him when the physio was about to leap into action, because a player had gone down, Cloughie would grab the poor guy, restraining him with: "Stay there, you go when I f****** tell you." And players would be left there, writhing on the ground, and Brian would shout over: "Come on, get up, we're down to ten men, you'll be ok, run it off." They soon got up and I suppose he was a bit contemptuous in certain situations. That's the background of how he would react to any player who transgressed his dictates and thus it was so with Johnny Metgod.

On one particular match day, from the first whistle, Johnny had been verbally haranguing the referee and inside ten minutes he was in the book. I noted immediately that Cloughie turned to Ronnie Fenton and said something which resulted in Ronnie shooting off down the tunnel, returning very quickly. Half-time came and as we all sat there Brian came in with an envelope which he stuck in Johnny Metgod's inside pocket. "That's for you." He proceeded to talk about the game for a couple of minutes before asking Johnny: "Have you read it yet? You can open it." So Johnny opened the envelope, looked at the contents and folded it before shoving it back into his pocket. It later transpired that Cloughie had got Ken Smales to write Johnny an official letter to say he was being fined half a week's wages, or something similar, for transgressing club rules in verbally harassing the referee. It was all done, typed up on club notepaper before half-time, waiting for Johnny.

I have only scratched the surface of Brian Clough. I've heard he regarded me as one of the best professional footballers he ever worked with and if that's true, what a testimonial. For me working with Brian Clough was a privilege and one of the most fortunate things to happen to me in a football lifetime.

Chapter 6

Portsmouth

I joined Portsmouth to add some experience, according to Alan Ball. After the fun and games Cloughie had engaged in at the end of my final Forest contract I spent most of that summer believing the chance of a move to Fratton Park had gone. Never the less I put a call in to Alan Ball to ask if Pompey were still interested. Fortunately they still wanted me and it didn't take long to wrap things up in time for pre-season training although there was almost a fall-out as we participated in the Isle of Man tournament.

A few top clubs used to participate in that pre-season event including Newcastle and Liverpool and we'd been there training for a few days when Bally asked me to do him a favour and go down to the airport and pick up Ron Yeats. I was staggered. Ron Yeats, a Liverpool legend, was coming over to watch some games and do some scouting for Pompey. Alan added that he was going to play some golf with Ron as well and I still couldn't believe that an Everton legend was asking me, a die-hard Evertonian, to meet up with, and escort to our hotel, an icon from across Stanley Park. I was getting the hump at such a suggestion and Alan noted that so tried to temper my angst with "oh he's a great laugh". I countered by telling my hero he had just burst my bubble asking me to look after someone Everton supporters used to hurl abuse at. But I took a taxi and spent the duration of the ride back exchanging stories of Merseyside football in the 1960s with a lovely, lovely man, even though he was a red, reminding him of the abuse he used to get from me and my mates on many a derby day. Even then he complimented me on the career I had enjoyed but all I could do was say it paled when compared with his and who would have thought it, certainly not me, if someone had suggested I would be sharing the company of two giants of Merseyside football, neither of them from Liverpool, but as Scouse as any born Scouser.

Having missed out on promotion the previous season Alan felt my experience could be a crucial factor in getting out of the Second Division. I had much to consider before I took on the challenge of a move at that stage of my life and my career. I was 33 and it was an upheaval uprooting my family and taking them to the other end of the country. But from a football perspective it was a great move for me and to get a two/three-year contract at that age was almost unheard of and Portsmouth even increased my salary. While Brian Clough saw me as "a deteriorating asset" with a decreasing salary to boot Alan Ball regarded me a bit more highly.

As well as the attraction of Portsmouth being promotion contenders over the two previous seasons there was the added pull of working under someone new, especially my boyhood idol. I also saw it as a challenge and I believe that if any footballer really wants to enjoy his football my advice would be to look for a challenge. Portsmouth were an ambitious club and they had some very good people behind them but they also had some very good players like Vince Hilaire, Billy Gilbert, Kevin Dillon, Kevin O'Callaghan and Noel Blake so it was always in my mind that we could do something with the squad. In that first year they also bought Mickey Quinn and he was a revelation, a true goalscorer.

Mickey was the most unlikely looking footballer and would be the first to admit the word ungainly summed him up but he was a wonderful personality and great to have about and great to be with. He was good company and if he displayed a casual, almost indifferent air, he didn't on the pitch. We got on very well, both being from Liverpool, and even today my wife reminds me of how much Quinny used to make her mother laugh. But his attitude often got him into trouble and none bigger than the time he went to prison.

He had been banned from driving but then foolishly got into his car and drove while that ban was current. The story went that his girlfriend was pregnant at that time and he had to rush her to hospital but was stopped by the police and it didn't take long for the ban to come to light. Consequently it went to court and cast a long shadow over pre-season training but we got on with it as did he. One day after training the players went for a quiet drink, as we could back then. We knew Mickey's case was on that afternoon and his fate was the hot topic. The general consensus was he would 'be ok with maybe a suspended sentence and/or a heavy fine' although one or two of us thought a spell inside wasn't impossible.

We hadn't been in the pub more than five minutes when we heard the news that Mickey had been sent down for three weeks. It was a blow for us so what he must have felt when the sentence was handed down goodness only knows. It was a foolish thing he did but the sentence did seem severe and there was a suspicion that the court was making an example of Mickey to send out a warning. From the football perspective not only would he be missing from the team he would also be unable to train and not be able to play immediately on release with the obvious knock-on effect on Portsmouth's promotion chances. He was a real goal threat and in the same way a goalkeeper can be so important to a team so too can a goalscorer and Mickey was just that to Pompey, as good as any in that league at the time. It was potentially a massive blow to our aspirations because the club was geared for progress, the chairman was a driving force and the fans were terrific so everything was in place.

I later heard that Mickey turned up at Winchester Prison in his designer Ralph Lauren suit and handmade Italian shoes. Inside it was alleged the following morning as Mickey was queuing with his bucket at slop-out time he was tripped from behind to loud shouts of "PENALTY REF" and at breakfast a shaven-headed inmate dropped a huge insect in his food and exclaimed "being a Scouser he must like beetles".

I remember driving past the prison one evening. I stopped and looked up at the lights shining through the rows of barred windows. I honestly felt for him and wondered what must be going through his mind. It's stating the obvious that it must have been a sobering experience for him.

Mickey got on with his sentence and when he was released it didn't seem to have affected his personality, on the outside at least. The only visible change was that he had shed a few pounds for which he was grateful. Alan Ball decided we would have a welcome back party for him. However appropriate or inappropriate it might have been we all thought it was a great idea because it must be placed on record that Portsmouth was a party club. Wimbledon and their Crazy Gang may have been the rogues and villains of the day and our rivals in that division but most of our players were south Londoners anyway and regarded themselves as Crazy Gang II.

We used to frequent a hotel called the Meon Valley Country Club. It was a regular haunt for a lot of us at Pompey and the manager was a Scouser, they get everywhere, indeed it is said Scousers get where water couldn't. So Alan Ball arranged a surprise homecoming party for Mickey at the hotel and when he was brought there, surreptitiously, he was greeted with miles of bunting and the drink flowed freely. The party lasted from mid-afternoon to well past midnight but we were back in training the next day and it didn't take Mickey long to get back to fitness but we still lost out to Wimbledon and missed promotion by three points. Needless to say that disappointment spurred us on the following year.

We began 1986/87 with a nine-game unbeaten run and were second in the table before losing our first game, 3-1, at Leeds. Ironically Andy Ritchie, who nearly joined Pompey, scored that day. Leeds would prove one of our fiercest competitors that season as would Derby County but we bounced back immediately following that defeat at Elland Road to beat Derby 3-1 at our place with a Mickey Quinn hat-trick. We followed up by beating West Brom to go top and never dropped out of the top two for the rest of the campaign. We were top going into Christmas and remained there until March when a goalless draw at Derby and a 1-1 draw at home to Leeds knocked us off the summit. We did go top again a couple of times before the end of the league programme but too many defeats, four in the last six fixtures, meant we finished second to Derby by six points.

One of the major factors in that promotion season was our defence, in which both myself and goalkeeper Alan Knight were ever-presents. We only conceded 11 goals at Fratton Park and away from home just 17 goals against in 21 games, the best in the division by a country mile, ten better than champions Derby. Another significant factor was the galvanising effect of the social aspect of the squad. It wasn't just a case of turning up for work, training and playing and that was it. The players mixed away from the club and truly enjoyed each other's company and it may seem glib to state this but although we partied hard we played hard and we trained hard also and our socialising never got in the way of the day job. We wouldn't allow that, individually or as a group.

Football is transient and footballers likewise. Players move in and move on for a variety of reasons but generally if there's an element of control players move upwards or at least sideways. Chelsea to Villa was a step up for me and the move to Forest I did not regard as anything but upwards because of the status of the club at the time. But my move to Portsmouth was, ostensibly, a start of downward momentum but it was sweetened by the aspect of a challenge and that challenge was to achieve promotion. And Portsmouth being on the coast added a bit of mystery because, like maybe Norwich, Carlisle and places like that, being so removed, on the periphery if you like, added a bit of siege mentality and that too had a galvanising effect. Away games from those places mentioned were truly away days and added to the bonding of the group. It was almost like being marooned but it helped if you grasped the positivity which the Pompey players did and it was a big honour for me to be captain of the promotion-winning side.

It was a funny one really because I had limited experience of being a skipper, just a few times at Villa. Mickey Kennedy was captain at Portsmouth and he must have been in the black book of every football assassin in the country. His reputation, fully justified, was fiery and fearsome. He would wind opponents up and often went over the top as far as physical challenges were concerned but I personally found him to be a genuine lad and he seemed to take to me as well to the point where for a good while I actually felt like his personal counsellor. Particularly at one point in time when he got embroiled in a couple of contentious newspaper articles which made people cringe. I knew it was serious when I got in to training on Monday morning and it was the hot topic of conversation having been all over the papers the day before. Naturally the p**s-taking targeted Mick the minute he walked through the door and he got slaughtered and despite all the raucous laughter directed at him it was obvious it was serious. I found I couldn't laugh with the others, maybe because of being at that senior stage of my career, and Mick could see that I wasn't joining in with the group.

Having used me as a bit of a barometer previously he pulled me aside after the jocularities had subsided and asked me what I thought of the whole episode and the articles. Before I could answer he spoke again, having seen the look on my face, and said: "You're not happy, are you?"

I smiled and told him it wasn't a case of my happiness, it was more a case of him being happy. He confirmed he wasn't particularly happy but I presumed he had been paid a few quid, to which he said it wasn't worth it, in hindsight. I could see the regret in his eyes and we tossed around a few of the implications of the articles including the worsening of his already blemished reputation. He might be secure in the knowledge that everyone in that Pompey dressing room would defend him but beyond Fratton Park it would be a different matter. I summed it all up by saying I wish he had spoken to me before agreeing to the articles.

I think Mick was under pressure anyway because of his fiery temperament which led to numerous bookings and inevitable suspensions which took his leadership out of our promotion drive. I think Alan Ball may have run out of patience with his skipper although Mick wasn't the only hothead in the team. Great characters though they were, there were a few short fuses in that dressing room and we could almost guarantee four or five of them would be suspended per year. I would never have subscribed to the theory that it was catching but I ended up with more bookings that season than at any other point in my career. Perhaps it was a case of being tarred by the same brush, an appropriately nautical term considering Portsmouth's naval history. As a defender you can probably bank on a couple of yellow cards a season but that campaign I think I was only one short of a first career suspension.

I have to say that as a manager Alan Ball never really stamped on indiscipline, maybe that was down to his own fiery temper and he perhaps thought he couldn't preach one thing having practised the complete opposite as a player. He was fairly lenient in that respect but Mick Kennedy was always walking a tightrope and you never knew what influences were behind some decisions at the club. Maybe the chairman had a quiet word with Alan, who knows, but the upshot was Bally made me captain. It was coming towards the end of the season and there were no hard feelings between me and Mick, we shared a drink and a chat about it and he had no problems about me taking the armband though I wasn't sure what he meant when he said I would be a better tosser than him. I think he was referring to the pre-kick-off formalities but you never knew with Mick.

It was an honour for me to captain Portsmouth and winning promotion added to that and there was a bit of a story near the end of the campaign which underlined our reputation as party animals. While Shrewsbury hosted Oldham in a midweek game I was doing a radio phone-in about Pompey who could secure promotion, without playing, given the right result that night. Shrewsbury were struggling near the foot of the table while Oldham were neck and neck with us vying for the second automatic promotion place so most people were expecting an Oldham victory. That was the most common thread of the questions the listeners were asking me and in between callers I was getting regular score flashes from Gay Meadow that did not fit in with general expectation. And just as the game was nearing the final whistle Shrewsbury, who had been leading 1-0, added a second goal through Dave Geddis, a former Villa colleague, to clinch victory. Not only did that knock Oldham out of the race for second place it confirmed promotion for Portsmouth without us kicking a ball that night. That was the signal, at around 9.20pm, for party time and in a hectic closing ten minutes of the show in between all the supporters' congratulatory calls I was saying: "I'm sure all the lads will be listening now, no, change that to, if any of you are listening get yourselves round to my house where the corks will be popping as soon as I get back. Give me 20 minutes."

We had an almighty all-night party and everyone was there including Bally and we had a great sing-song and knees-up accompanied by copious amounts of alcohol because they could drink, as was the case with most clubs those days but, as with most clubs, we were out on the training ground the next day or later that day actually. There wasn't a drink culture in football then. I regarded it more as a hydration culture, the beginning of the hydration strategy we have today. That's my sticking and I am storying to it!

Because of the era and the culture of football at the time I don't think the players themselves would allow the drinking to affect their professional attitude, in most cases certainly. It wasn't so much it being a drink culture because we've always had that in this country; it was more the work ethic and what was expected. It really was a case of a fair day's pay for a fair day's work. Managers knew what went on but players were fully aware that you had to be fit enough for training for the next session whether it was the following morning or even a few hours later. Work hard and play hard was the semi-official motto, for footballers in general, and certainly those at Fratton Park. I truly believe that if it were physiologically possible, some of that squad did have hollow legs.

There was one episode when things did go a little over the top and it left me thinking there was taking a drink and taking the proverbial by drinking at lunchtime then afterwards and then in the evening. I maintained a bit of distance from that philosophy because although I was the senior pro and the rest of the players were younger than me they had been together as a group long before I arrived. But there was one instance where Alan Ball had asked me to take training before a game. We were away from home and after we had arrived at our hotel the lads obviously had a drink or several and the next morning it showed. So I decided to set up a specific training session based upon heading and testing the back four players by loading in crosses for which the forwards would challenge aerially too. The players who were worse for wear were mainly the central defenders who, in my opinion, had overindulged. In between thumping their headers as far as they could manage I could hear them cursing me but I wasn't sympathetic. My argument was that if that didn't teach them a lesson nothing would.

In fairness to the Pompey lads they never let themselves or the club down and epitomised the team ethic as well as the work ethic. There's a lot of talk these days about when a manager loses the dressing room and it does have substance. There are many aspects to a football club but everything at a club is built on the ethos of the dressing room, it is the heartbeat of a club. Yes the supporters are crucial but they follow the fortunes that emanate from what is produced by the players on the park and that derives from the ethos of the dressing room. Managers and coaches know the importance of a strong dressing room and the most successful teams have one, they have to. And when things don't quite go to plan, maintaining equilibrium is paramount.

It was something that emerged as our First Division campaign began and gathered a damaging momentum as we got deeper and deeper into the league programme, which rapidly became a fight for survival. We only picked up one point from the first four fixtures, a

2-2 draw at home to Southampton. In the three defeats we shipped another 13 goals and were 20th in a division of 21 by the time we recorded a win in the final game of August, 2-1 at home to West Ham. It was a shock to our system because Alan Ball during the summer had bought quite a few new players. With it being Pompey's first top-flight campaign for nearly 30 years the owner John Deacon had invested quite a bit of money but there was a far from seamless integration of the new players into our club.

There was a special team spirit at Fratton Park, a bond between the players that was quite unique and we were used to one another. To bring in players to strengthen the squad was one thing but to bring in so many players in such a short space of time and expect an immediate blending of the incoming with those already there was unrealistic. Players who had been part of the team for a long time suddenly found themselves out of the picture and the whole process became very disruptive and that had an effect on the team with a consequent knock-on effect on the park because of the way it affected the players who had been there for years, players who had taken the club up. Even I felt a bit put out despite being there a short time.

Change is inevitable, it's as much a part of football as winning and losing, but it's the manner in which change is effected that is key. The culture of a club is down to the manager and the infrastructure he creates and part of that culture is the grafting of incoming players into that club, and I think it didn't work at Portsmouth then and I wasn't alone amongst the incumbent squad. That isn't meant as a criticism of the players who came in, it was hard for them. It was difficult to come into a new culture and for them to win their spurs and that is another important part of football for me.

When a player goes from one club to another expecting everything to fall neatly into place because of his status or ego it is pure folly. Any status he earned at his previous club was exactly that, earned. You have to earn acceptance, earn your spurs, wherever you are in football, each and every time. It's as basic as that. It's the same in any job but even more so in a results-driven industry. A player can come with a reputation but at Pompey there were too many players relying on their status and for the first time ever I got a feeling of two different groups within the squad. That can be divisive but it depends on the personalities involved. There wasn't the rancour normally associated with a 'them and us situation', it was just a feeling. It was just as hard for the new players if it wasn't working for them and they were out of the team they would be scratching their head wondering what they were doing there. But it was different for the players who had been at the club a while, if they were in and out of the side, because they had already earned their spurs. I suppose established squad members had earned the right to be aggrieved at not playing because they had already made their contribution whereas the newcomers had to earn their right to bellyache first.

Whatever the explanation there was disharmony and it proved a significant factor in some very poor results because of the difficulty of moulding a new team spirit at the club from the two factions. Making the step up from Second Division to First Division was difficult enough but statistics do not lie, particularly at the end of the season, which was really a culmination of a poor campaign that started badly and didn't improve.

We never recovered from a poor start and we were losing games to teams we really should not have been losing to, all season. The hammerings we suffered at the hands of Arsenal, Liverpool and Manchester United were to a degree understandable but, with all due respect, 4-2 to Oxford, who would be relegated with us, and some of the other teams, we should have done better with the players we had.

The 4-0 defeat at Anfield was significant because it signalled to me that we were facing a season of struggling, and it was only the tenth league game, only one quarter of the campaign gone. And yet, as was so often the case that season, we started the game so well in glorious October sunshine. I also remember that day for something that happened prior to kick-off.

In those days we didn't have the structured warming up that goes on today and most players had their own particular way of preparing to play. As I got into the twilight years of my career my warm-up consisted of running. I would start with a couple of slow laps around the pitch. I would jog around the perimeter, cutting across the six-yard box, not around the back of the goals. It was only about 45 minutes before kick-off so there was a fair crowd inside Anfield already, meaning I was subjected to loads of booing and jeering particularly at the Kop end. I'd like to state I was blissfully unaware of the derision and my only thought was hoping there weren't Liverpool people there thinking who's this Evertonian winding us up. I suppose it did look out of the ordinary with the two teams warming up at either end of the pitch with a solo jogger doing his own thing. I decided I wasn't going to not do my own warm-up just because it was Anfield. That was my routine and I was sticking to it.

After the two jogs around the pitch I moved up a gear and did some medium stretches, 50 yards each, before finishing with some shuttle sprints to work up the necessary sweat to start the game. I was really lathered and I went back into our dressing room, about 15 minutes before kick-off. Almost immediately I was followed by Paul Mariner. He was the driest of wits at the best of times but on that occasion, with an amalgam of northern and cockney humour, he waltzed over spouting "f*** me Swainey, they're taking the p**s aren't they". "What?" I asked. He said: "I've just been out there doing my warm up and there's four of their lads on deck-chairs on the edge of their box, knotted handkerchiefs and some flasks. Are they 'aving a larf, do they think they're in for an easy afternoon or what." I was doubled up laughing like the rest of us but in all seriousness whenever I used to play at Liverpool all I ever got at Anfield was a kick up the arse and a bottle of warm Higson's Brown Ale. Indeed any player would be pleased if he could say "I got over the halfway line once at Liverpool" because it was such a formidable place.

Although we lost 4-0 that day we actually started well and Liverpool only led 1-0 at half-time and that goal came late on. I foolishly thought we could be on for a point but in the second half a collapse occurred and it wasn't the first time and would not be the last. So for me that was the start of doubting we could survive that season. Trying to gel too may players too soon wasn't working and as early as the first game in October I felt we would struggle. We conceded 22 by the end of the tenth game and it was to prove no better at the other end.

We struggled for goals that season with not a single player reaching double figures in the league. Kevin Dillon finished up as leading scorer with nine, but four of those were penalties and even Mickey Quinn could only manage eight, from 29 games, so as the campaign progressed if we went a goal down the immediate thought was "where is a goal going to come from?"

As the results got worse so did my inner feeling that things were looking ominous. I don't know how the new lads were feeling because some of them weren't getting a game but it was bleak as far as the players who got us promotion were concerned and that sort of feeling is contagious. It was also a difficult time for me personally because I was nearly 36 and conscious that the club would be looking to bring in younger players so when we slipped into the bottom four and then lost 4-0 to Forest it was a bleak winter in prospect on several levels. Little did we know, although the suspicion grew as the points total did not, we would not get out of the bottom quartet for the remainder of the season.

I recall being out of the team as we began the New Year with a home game against Arsenal. I was watching from the stand, not even on the bench, having been 'bombed' by Bally. Naturally I was down but I do remember David Rocastle being brilliant for Arsenal that day. He was outstanding. I obviously didn't watch too many games from the stand but he got me off my seat for probably the first time ever. His play was effortless and there was one instance following a Pompey attack when he picked the ball up just outside the Arsenal box. He then sidestepped one challenge, then another and another and next thing he's made it to our penalty area and because he was such a wonderful mover with the ball, none of our players could get anywhere near him. He finished by smashing the ball just wide of the goal. It was such a wonderful passage of play by David, almost Messi-like. It brought me to my feet and I wasn't alone. Such a quality player and what a tragedy he died so young aged just 33.

When I think back to that time it puts into perspective my anger at being dropped. Being dropped at any time is not good but it hurt a bit more for two reasons. It was the first time I was dropped at Portsmouth and I had been left out by Alan Ball. I spent two-and-a-half years at Portsmouth and it was a wonderful experience to play under my boyhood hero. I had a great relationship with Alan but when he left me out of the team to face Arsenal I felt especially affronted.

While he was a good manager I felt he struggled to handle real pressure which may seem strange to some because he handled pressure so well during a very successful high level playing career. It was almost like he wasn't really a man-manager but more of a players' manager because he found it difficult to make some decisions. He was probably too much of a players' manager and I can be so categorical in stating that having worked with Brian Clough and Ron Saunders, who were vastly different personalities to Alan. I can see why it worked for Brian and Ron and why it never worked for Bally. He had some talented players at Portsmouth but having been a cavalier player himself he was also a cavalier manager. That was his nature, he was flamboyant, and he liked to be close to the players, didn't want to upset anyone and you cannot do that as a manager and it probably took me 18 months to realise that.

He also seemed to suffer from a lack of self-confidence, as a manager. He would ask me how Cloughie would handle a particular situation and I told him of a few episodes at Forest and some of Brian's methods of dealing with certain incidents. Alan lapped it up and was intrigued by some of those methods so when he dropped me it wasn't how I thought it would happen, I thought he could have done it differently, better, for both of us. It was done, dusted and brushed under the carpet so quickly. I felt there was no communication and that situation existed for a couple of weeks until I came back into the side for the Oxford United game and I remember having a pop at him for not a single word passing between us from me being left out and being selected to face Oxford.

We were in the dressing room and he said something to me in passing. I can't remember what it was but it caused me to snap back at him, saying something like "that's the first time you've spoken to me for two weeks". That retort hit him but it also hit me. Call it egotism, call it petulance, poor communication, I don't know. It was just my response to what had happened and it was clear, to me anyway, that my time at the club was drawing to an end and fortunately I was able to get away, on loan, at West Brom which was probably timely or so I felt at that time. But even that opportunity wasn't relayed to me by my manager, it was left to one of his backroom staff. The whole episode underlined my view that Alan Ball, manager, didn't actually manage the task of telling people very well. I came away from the experience of being dropped by him bitter, sour and, dare I say it, with my silly ego a bit bruised and our relationship also suffered a bit of bruising that wouldn't go away for many years.

I got some respite from the tension between us through my loan spell at The Hawthorns. It proved a breath of fresh air and the future began to look a bit more promising but I was recalled by Bally and back into the side for another thrashing, 4-1 at Luton. I really didn't want to go back but to be fair to Alan we did try to build bridges a little. The club's situation was too desperate for anyone to be more important than collective effort so personalities had to be put aside. All the players recognised we were in serious trouble and grasping at straws. We were trying to beg a goal, beg a point and I remember each and every realisation that the situation was getting worse game after game, vividly, until relegation was confirmed.

I remained in the side until the final game when Paul Hardyman returned from injury but things didn't improve and we only managed one win in that spell, 1-0 at Spurs. It was like a dark cloud hanging over us but made worse for me by virtue of the fact that I was at the end of my contract and 36-years-old. I knew I was in the final furlong as a player but there wasn't even any consolation thinking back to previous successes I enjoyed. We had been relegated and it was there in the cold light of day, in the record books, we were losers, we had lost our right to be a top-flight club. If we had survived, even by one point, what an achievement that would have been to survive a season-long dogfight but we didn't. For Bally it was really the first setback in a managerial career that had been quite successful at Portsmouth.

More than 20 years later I attended a game at Villa Park where I bumped into Jimmy Case. I had already heard that Alan's wife had been ill. My wife and I had got to know them well at Portsmouth and when I spoke to Jimmy, who still lived on the South Coast, I was already aware that Leslie was deteriorating. I hadn't spoken to Alan since I left Pompey so I had that parting on my conscience.

I say it was on my conscience because I don't think people should be that way. People can get bitter and egotistical about things. My mind drifted back to more than two years of a wonderful time when I was playing for my hero, fantastic fun and a great relationship between us but I allowed all that good stuff to be affected by a few months when my pride was bruised by being left out of the side. Let's be honest I was, after all, an ageing player at the time we were heading for the First Division so why wasn't it appropriate for me to feel as I did. Of course that wasn't how I felt then hence my throwing of the toys out of the pram. Meeting up with Jimmy stirred all those feelings and memories, and there was also a large measure of regret, so I got Alan's number from Jimmy. When I got home that night it was quite late and everyone else had gone to bed so I poured myself a drink and rang

Bally. Leslie answered the phone and it was like the clock had been turned back and everything was normal. She asked about Lily and the kids and we had a good chat before she said she'd go and tell Alan I was on the phone.

"Hello kid, how are you, how you doin' Swainey, ok?" came that familiar squeaky voice from all those years before. We chatted and I asked him about Leslie, saying she sounded fantastic. Then I heard him walk over and close the door before coming back to me and saying that she wasn't well and hadn't been for a while and was just putting on a brave face. We started talking football and before I knew it something like 90 minutes had passed and we had covered every subject from the state of the game today to foreign players, bemoaning the lack of good pros while telling me I had been a "great pro to work with". I admit that it was quite an emotional conversation and I was almost tearful.

After we finished talking I came off the phone feeling absolved I suppose, and really glad I'd phoned him for a catch-up. I thought if I hadn't had that conversation with him it would have been such a shame. And with him passing away just a few years back I would never have got the chance to clear the air between us, not that there was any bad feeling on his part but it convinced me that you shouldn't hold grudges, life's too short. It's not that I avoided talking to him over the years but football, and life, is like that. People go their separate ways and lead busy lives and don't go out of their way to ring and I'm the same. I don't go out of my way to call people unless there's a reason but I went out of my way to ring Alan that night because of the circumstances in his life at that time.

I loved everything about Pompey, the city, the location and the people and I guess the thing about the place that really appealed to me was that I thought it was a northern football city, plonked on the South Coast. It was a bit of a cosmopolitan area and being a port as well gave it another synergy with my home town of Liverpool. I really felt at home there.

Chapter 7

Crewe Alexandra

They do say what goes around comes around and that was true in my case, joining Crewe Alexandra at an age when most professional footballers are retired. And the football world really is a small place where you bump into the same people over and over again.

Dario Gradi was instrumental in me becoming a professional footballer and when I was nearing the end of my three-year contract at Portsmouth he re-entered my life. I was out of the side and Ron Atkinson, the West Brom manager, wanted me on loan. I spoke to Ron who outlined his need for some experienced players as the team was near the foot of the table and he invited me to join 'the bus-pass brigade', Andy Gray, Paul Dyson, Tony Morley, and Brian Talbot, even suggesting signing me in would "send the average age rocketing".

I went to West Brom for a couple of months and Ron was very good in allowing me to stay down south and only travel up for training on Thursday and Friday before playing the Saturday game and returning home on Saturday night. He would allow me Monday, Tuesday and Wednesday off, unless we had a midweek game. I had a great time under Ron and enjoyed myself at a good club with good people. But at my age I knew I wasn't going to remain at Portsmouth so my mind was mulling over what lay ahead.

Albion were struggling around the relegation zone when I arrived but over my eight-week loan period we managed to turn it around and moved up the table. Before I went back to Portsmouth, just before the end of the season, Ron Atkinson said he would try and do a deal for me during the summer, which was great. We had gone from the Midlands so going back would suit all the family.

I enjoyed working for Ron. For all the reputation he cultivated he was interesting to work under. He was another character in my career and was as he was portrayed, larger than life. It was an image he played up to and actively encouraged and I liked him. He was good company and always ready with a quip or a joke but he was quite serious about football and winning and was a fellow Scouser.

Back at Pompey the inevitable happened and we were relegated, however that was softened by a bonus from West Brom for helping them avoid the drop. It wasn't huge but a nice gesture and all I had to do was wait for Ron to come and arrange a deal to take me back to the Albion. But time went on and no word was forthcoming from Ron and the more that time dragged on the more I felt let down because I had pinned my hopes on returning there as there was no future for me at Portsmouth. So I joined hundreds of other footballers, who were on the list issued by the PFA at the end of every season, looking for a club. It is a stark reality to see your name on that list on which every name is waiting for a call. But I wasn't prepared to wait so I rang Ron.

I asked him what was happening but as soon as the first words came out of his mouth in response I smelled a rat. He went on about having to shift one or two players before he could bring anyone in. So I knew I couldn't put all my eggs in Ron's basket and as if by fate Dario, who I hadn't spoken to for years, rang me out of the blue. He said he had seen my name on the list and, after exchanging the usual pleasantries, came the invite. He said: "You know we have a good set-up here at Crewe which has been going well for six or seven years. I know you've always wanted to stay in the game and coach or manage so do you fancy coming here? I'm not really looking for a player but I could do with a coach and there's a job going here as youth coach but you can carry on playing as well because you are still very fit."

I agreed with Dario I still had some mileage in my legs and life in my lungs, so wasn't ready to swap football boots for a zimmer frame. However I did understand that some managers would look at my age and pretty much base their assessment on that, whatever I thought, but not Dario Gradi. It was the best of both worlds because he wanted me to continue playing while I could test the waters as far as coaching was concerned with one of the best in the business. He proposed that I stay on a player's wage but my title was player-coach.

I travelled to see Dario knowing little of Crewe as a club or as Dario used to refer to them "regular relegation candidates", but he was proud he could change that to "we've turned things around and now have a good set-up". I could see that but I was soon faced with the reality of a massive drop in salary. That's not so much of a problem if it was like nowadays and going down from £50,000 a week to £25,000. It was more like going down from several hundred to a couple of hundred and I had my family to consider. Never the less it was on the table and a fantastic opportunity for me to take my first tentative steps towards coaching. I knew deep down I couldn't say no to Crewe. There was also the feeling that I owed Dario for getting me into the game so I didn't feel I could make a big issue regarding finance. As I saw it I could still play a bit and learn my trade as a coach alongside Dario. I couldn't see any better place to start.

We were very fortunate to sell up in Hampshire as quickly as we did because there was a property slump at the time. It was a time of upheaval on the personal side too. Inside 18 months my mother died, my mother-in-law died and my son Tom was born so in many respects we decided that going back to Liverpool was for the best and we settled in the south of the city and stayed there long enough to get Tom into a good school, which was a major priority. Locating where we did made commuting into Crewe very simple as I could get the train into Crewe Station which as most people know is right next to Gresty Road, just a short walk from the platforms. Driving wasn't a problem either so it was a good move.

I immersed myself into the job at Crewe but it didn't take long to realise it was growing arms and legs with the responsibilities and expectations, particularly from Dario who is steeped in football. When I first went to Chelsea I thought I was football daft but listening to people like Dario and Dave Sexton and the way football consumed their lives I knew I was a novice in that respect. I had to face the fact that the demands at Crewe were going to be more than I had ever been used to and something I had to get to grips with, fast.

That realisation brought the commuting into question because that was proving prohibitive in terms of time. I was sometimes coaching in the evening after coaching the youth team in the afternoon having done my own training with the first team earlier in the day. I could sometimes be at the ground, working, until 7.30pm or 8pm before jumping on the train back to Liverpool and getting home past 10pm, by which time Tom would be asleep and I would only get to see him briefly in the morning before school. So we decided it was best on all fronts to move and we relocated to the Nantwich area.

The job continued to grow apace and I was getting stuck in more and more and it became all-consuming. On the field we were quite successful and by December we clinched top spot with a 2-1 win at Rotherham. They were one of our main rivals that season, along with Tranmere, and would eventually win the Fourth Division title, four points ahead of us and two ahead of Rovers.

Crewe were in the top two for a couple of months but three consecutive defeats in the spring knocked us down to fourth. We recovered and five points from our last three games clinched third place and promotion, which was far more than I expected. It made me realise there was more to football than winning the European Cup. You could achieve other things which was of growing importance to me like pushing oneself and others too on to greater things. I had achieved promotion with Chelsea and with Portsmouth and had success at Villa but you can't win things all the time. There aren't many winners around. You can only have one league winner, one FA Cup winner etc.

To help a club like Crewe get into the Third Division, for the first time in 20 years and to help Portsmouth get back into the top-flight for the first time in 30 years, were major achievements. I didn't see them as personal achievements but as club milestones, something all involved could be part of and they gave me a tingle. I played 40 games in the first team that season and with my coaching responsibilities on top it made it a very full first year with Crewe Alexandra. But then an opportunity came up at West Brom where Brian Talbot became manager. Naturally I told Dario who asked me what I was going to do so I said I wanted to speak to them. The Albion wanted me as a coach not as a player. They were in the Second Division at the time so my playing days would have been over at that level.

I came back from talks at The Hawthorns and told Dario I wanted to take the job. He wished me good luck but then outlined his Crewe plans for the following year and his hopes that they could stay in the Third Division. He added that the youth coach was leaving so there would be more scope for me but if I wanted to go then that was fine.

My mind was set on West Brom and a new start but a couple of days later Brian Talbot rang me and told me he couldn't do the deal we had discussed. He said he could still offer me the job but not on the terms agreed. I told Brian I had already informed Dario I was leaving. He reiterated I could still have the job but not the agreed money. It was all looking a bit stupid to me. I had never really been caught up in that kind of thing in football. Everything had usually been straight and rock-solid and the people I worked for had been likewise.

I don't know why Brian had moved the goalposts and I naturally expressed my great annoyance to him as well as my embarrassment. So I had to stew overnight at the prospect of going back to Dario the next day and telling him I wasn't going to Albion. When I told him he just said "that's what happens in football". Thankfully he added my job was still there so I got stuck in with renewed vigour. That lasted about six months then I rather foolishly began to feel I was more ready than I had been when the Albion chance came, or more prepared would be more accurate. How wrong I was because with hindsight, I know now I was nowhere near ready despite my confidence. That maybe explains my hesitation in taking the next opportunity. Never the less, even now, I regret not taking the chance to manage Wycombe.

Apart from the attraction of taking my first steps into management there was the obvious pull of becoming manager of a club where I had once played. There were still a lot of people there from my time, including the guy who had signed me for Wycombe, Brian Lee, who by then was a director. I rang him as I had heard they were looking for a manager. Brian asked me if I would be interested and when I said yes it was decided I would put in an application. Within a couple of days Brian told me the chairman wanted to speak with me, on a Sunday. That slotted in perfectly for me as we were playing Fulham, on 27th January 1990, at Craven Cottage, on the Saturday, so I told Dario I was going across to speak to Wycombe and wouldn't be travelling back on the team coach. Dario was ok with that but asked who I was going to speak with. I couldn't tell him because all I knew was that I was going for a chat with club officials.

I arrived at Adams Park for what I thought was an informal chat with the chairman and Brian Lee and discovered it was a full-blown interview. The first clue was me being directed to a corridor where I witnessed a smartly dressed guy emerging from a room, shaking hands with another guy and saying "we'll be in touch", before inviting me into the same room. I recognised several faces from my time at Wycombe, including the chairman and Brian.

Straight away the chairman began with his plans and those of the club and what they wanted from their manager. They spread huge blueprints for the new stadium in front of me and the whole package was impressive as was the club's ambition to gain promotion from the Conference. My role was to include the founding of a new youth system in tandem with bringing in players of good enough quality to progress the club to the point where the youth system would bear fruit and they would take up the challenge. They were most complimentary about my grounding under Dario and my playing career and painted a very rosy picture though we never discussed terms. For my part not going there expecting an interview threw me a little and I found myself saying things like "whatever you do and whoever you appoint make sure it's the right fellah for the job because this all looks a very exciting prospect for the club". I told them I still had fond memories of my time there and it all seemed so informal that I didn't feel I was being interviewed. The whole process lasted no more than 45 minutes and we shook hands and off I went.

When I got home I told Lily how things had gone and how as things unfolded it began to feel more like an interview than a chat but I still wasn't certain. I told her that I would fancy the job if it were offered me but added that there had been a couple of dozen applicants and they had interviewed six or seven. The next morning, around 8.30am, the phone rang and it was Ivor Beeks, the Wycombe chairman. He banged on for a couple of minutes about how keen a number of people were to take the job but that he and the board were unanimous that I would be "the right person to manage the club". I, rather casually, responded with "ok" and Ivor said they wanted me to start as soon as possible and stated that things like salary, budgets etc would be discussed when I came down.

They wanted to make an announcement the following day and hold a press conference on the Wednesday. Still taken aback at the pace things were moving I agreed, adding that although I was excited about their plans I still had to speak to Dario. They asked me to get back to them before the end of the day and I agreed. I was certainly beginning to realise more strongly than ever that this was a good opportunity with good prospects. Crewe were only getting gates of two or three thousand and there seemed much greater potential at Wycombe. Although they were a non-league club, when they got into the Football League they could really take off.

I went to see Dario and outlined what had happened and told him I had been offered the job and that I was going to take it. But then he reined me in a bit and proceeded to ask some searching but very valid questions. "Who was I going to have as my assistant?" When I told him I would inherit someone Dario responded by saying that person had been there for 20 or 30 years. Then he asked if I could bring my own assistant in and I truthfully didn't know and hadn't even given it any thought. So it seemed I was stuck with the chap already there but Dario told me I should really look into that for clarification. He then asked who was going to do all my scouting. I didn't know and Dario emphasised how important that was, adding: "I know if it was me I would go and get Barry Fry because he is the best in non-league and the competition for players is intense at that level."

The barrage of questions became more intense and Dario asked what would happen if Wycombe didn't get promotion into the Football League at the end of the first year. "We'll try again the year after." "And what if you don't get up then because only one team goes up from the Conference? If you're lucky they'll stick with you but halfway through the following season if it's not looking good for promotion they won't keep faith too much longer and you'll be out on your arse, anyway what's the rush?"

I tried to emphasise what a good opportunity it was but Dario reminded me that Crewe had been in the Fourth Division a year earlier and how I was watching non-league games for him, seeking players. He said if I was going to manage in non-league I would end up scouting Sunday football for players. He concluded by saying that because of the level I had been used to I wouldn't be able to stand for that kind of set-up. I'd get a player ringing up to say he can't make it because he has to pick the kids up for example, one of the pitfalls of part-time football. Obviously we never had that situation at Crewe because the players were professional, they had to be there because they were being paid.

After pointing out all the negatives Dario said: "Look Ken, it must be bad enough being here at this level so you really need to give this some serious thought. There's no rush, is it money? We can offer you a raise." And he threw a figure at me which represented a 25% increase but I told him it wasn't the money. When he asked what Wycombe were offering me, financially, I obviously didn't know because we hadn't discussed it yet. "You don't even know your contract, you don't even know if it's one or two years? I tell you, there's too many uncertainties here and this needs serious consideration by you. By the way you've always got a job here. As long as I am here you are here if you want to be." Then, as if by magic the chairman John Bowler walked in. Dario turned to me and suggested I tell Wycombe I would let them know by the end of the week. When I said I couldn't he said "they'd do that to you, you really need some time to think this over".

Dario had really given me the wobbles and a lot more to think of than when I first walked into his office that day. Maybe it was my character, maybe I should have been bolder or maybe he should have encouraged me to take the opportunity, the sort that doesn't come around too often. He said if I was in football for the long haul it would be a good idea to give myself the best chance of longevity, adding: "Managers come and go but if you can coach you will always be in demand. There are more coaching jobs around than manager's jobs so if you don't succeed as a manager it's bloody difficult so you have to be careful with your choices."

The chairman then endorsed what Dario said and agreed with him that if it was security I needed I would always have a job at Crewe. He also confirmed the pay rise Dario had mooted. I went away and gave it some serious thought then I rang Wycombe and told them I wouldn't be taking the job. I told them it was a great job, the right job but it was at the wrong time for me. But the moment those words came out of my mouth, and indeed the next day, I was telling myself such an opportunity might not come again because I genuinely thought it was a job that had prospects. Ivor Beeks was very understanding and thanked me for coming down to interview and wished me well for the future. Two days later Martin O'Neill got the job then I indulged in some more self-administered doses of angst that I should have taken it. I felt like that for many, many years, and still do sometimes.

I put it behind me and got on with the job at Crewe where I spent a total of six years and it gave me a brilliant insight into coaching as well as close-up experience of the conveyor-belt of young talent that emerged from Crewe Alexandra, from David Platt to Dean Ashton, to make that club, arguably, the most highly regarded for producing young footballers, as well as being the most highly respected coach in Dario Gradi. With the benefit of hindsight the grounding I received was priceless. Dario is a self-confessed better coach than a talent spotter or scout. However he has always had a good eye for talent. As a coach, a thinker and an innovator he is one of the best in the country. He had the same 100% conviction as Dave Sexton and you must have that if you want to succeed at the highest level.

Dario could go from coaching the Under-14s on the Astroturf pitch outside the changing rooms, walking off soaking with sweat, and into the first team group ready to deliver his team talk to the players who were going out for a league game ten minutes later. That's what he did, morning, noon and night and he did it seamlessly, from young teens to old pros. From simple, football basics to a strategic, tactical game plan on which points and livelihoods depended and he's been doing it for decades. And, win, lose or draw, he would still be philosophical at the end of the day. He would always look for the positives and, for example, could be heard to mutter something along the lines of "well, we've a couple of Under-14s who will be ok in a couple of years" and that always pleased him. He always looked at the bigger picture but still managed to know every single player at the club and could give an on-the-spot appraisal of each one of them because he coached every single player and he would always stop and make time to have a word. And when I looked at how things were at other places I worked where work got partitioned off, Dario did the lot.

Because we both coached at all levels it brought me into contact with players a lot younger than me and even when playing for the first team I was the old man of the bunch. Playing with kids years junior to me was an experience, especially for the first few years at the club and players like Rob Jones, Craig Hignett and Steve Walters. When we had moved back to Liverpool I would often pick Craig up and drive in with him. Then when he was driving he would occasionally chauffeur me.

Dario's forte was picking up players from other clubs who didn't quite make it and polishing their talent and when he'd done that and taken them as far as he could, if he had coaxed their potential out and beyond Crewe, they moved up the football ladder. The list is a long one and has a lot of names on it that went on to play international football and the case of Rob Jones is typical of that scenario.

When Liverpool came in for Rob, aged just 19, he already had 75 league games under his belt having made his Crewe debut at 16, so Dario wasn't going to stand in his way and keep him another 40-odd games. Rob was ready to make the step up and so he did, effortlessly. And there is a connection there because on 5th November 1991 I became the oldest Crewe Alexandra first team player, aged 39 years and 281 days, when I took the field for my only game that season, at home to Maidstone United. I replaced Rob Jones, a full 20 years my junior, who was the regular full-back and that game was on his birthday to boot. Only Rob wasn't there because he had joined Liverpool and I took him there.

A few weeks earlier I had gone into Gresty Road where it was a hive of activity with the club secretary Gill Palin dashing in and out of Dario's office. Dario asked me to do him a favour and take Rob Jones over to Liverpool because Crewe had just agreed to his transfer and they wanted him over at Anfield to sign his contract.

On the journey over Rob was a bag of nerves, talking 20 to the dozen. He was asking me what I thought and I could feel the excitement in him and was trying to imagine what it would have been like for me at that age going over to sign for a massive club like Liverpool. He wanted to know everything that was going to happen so I explained there would be a medical, probably just a straightforward physical and the contract will probably be as straightforward. Then he asked what he should ask for and I said: "I don't think you should ask for anything because they'll give you what they think is right for you at this stage of your career and while you've had a lot of games for Crewe this is a whole different level." I put it bluntly and asked if Liverpool offered him a pay rise of £50 a week would he turn it down? His "no" ended that particular aspect of the conversation.

I also told him that while he had been a Crewe first team regular he would have to get his head around the fact that he was going to a club where he was likely to be a regular in the reserve team but even at that level he would be surrounded by international footballers who couldn't get into the Liverpool first team. What did I know? Less than 48 hours later Graeme Souness tossed the kid into his debut, and not just any debut. He was pitted against Ryan Giggs, at Old Trafford, kept him in his pocket, was voted man of the match and before the season was over he was capped by England. His last game for Crewe was against Gillingham!

There were so many talented players at Crewe while I was there and Rob would probably have been just about the most talented in terms of realising his potential but Steve Walters was another excellent footballer and he became the youngest ever Crewe player when he made his debut aged just 16. Great things were expected of Steve, who was not unlike Arsenal's Jack Wilshere. He was a similar body shape and good with both feet, had a good feel for the ball and was able to deliver a pass with great precision and weighting. He was also a fearless competitor and maybe he should have gone further than he did but unfortunately he suffered a lot of injury problems. But it's there in the record books just how many players Dario brought through at Crewe and over such a long period of time.

I often wondered how he managed to do that so often, year after year. I would hear him talking to other people, reporters or parents and they would ask the same question and he would always point to his elbow and say "it's elbow grease and the work you do with them". Of course there was also the major attraction or 'carrot' that Dario could dangle in front of a youngster he wanted to sign. He could say to a youngster: "If you're good enough you could be in our first team at 16 or 17. If you go to United or another big club you won't." There was no guarantee but as the years went by enough players did just that and ended up at bigger clubs, with dozens of league games under their belt, for it to prove that starting at Crewe was a good stepping stone, as Rob Jones showed. Their decision-making ability would certainly be more advanced via the first team playing experience gained and that unfortunately is one of the criticisms levelled at Academy players now, that if they stay in that system too long, at Under-16, Under-18 level, with the odd reserve game, what experience is that when set against getting someone out on loan, playing with men and enhancing decision-making capability, on and off the field and learning about winning, losing and everything football comprises?

To be fair Dario was always realistic about a player's ability and his potential and that approach has benefitted me. It is something which has stood me in good stead in the job I do with England Youth players in terms of potential and understanding the issues of growth, opportunities and challenges. The grounding I received at Crewe has probably been more beneficial for me in recent years than it was 15 years ago, perhaps summed up by something Dario regularly said to me if I commented after a game that a certain player wasn't doing this or that or wasn't doing it quick enough. Dario would turn to me and say: "Well, if he was doing it he wouldn't be here playing for us."

Chapter 8

Management

By the time the manager's job at Wigan Athletic came around, in 1993, I truly felt ready for the next phase of my career. I arranged to meet with Stephen Gage, the Wigan chairman, in Sandbach where I was living then. I arrived at the designated meeting point at 7pm. Twenty minutes later there was no sign of my prospective new boss. At 7.30pm I rang home to ask if he had been in touch. I had no mobile phone then. My mood was not good and I told Lily, "this is a joke".

I was beginning to get cold feet and ready to walk until the hotel receptionist came and said there was a call for me from Stephen Gage. He rattled off a completely plausible excuse of "traffic problems on the M6" and swore blind he would be with me in 20 minutes so I mumbled something, put the phone down and waited. Eventually he walked in hot and bothered because it was May and very warm. When he inquired where we could sit I said anywhere as the place is now empty.

We sat down and he spoke first: "Look Kenny, first things first, the job is yours." "I should think so after keeping me waiting for two hours" was, I think, a quite restrained reply. If the first thing he had said was "ok Kenny let's talk" I think I would have told him to get lost, so I became manager of Wigan Athletic there and then.

The chairman proceeded to go through the squad with his assessment of them, individually. I told him I was already aware of the players, including the 35-year-old centre-back he was trying to foist upon me. I thought it prudent to nod and mumble assent at what I considered appropriate junctures and that seemed to work. He then outlined finance which was an education in itself.

The outlay on wages was between £5,000 and £5,200 per week and he told me I could have ten players earning around £500 a week, though he did add: "But that might leave you a bit short." Conversely I could have a really big squad "earning £250 a week each". Both were ludicrous but that was the remit. He then moved on to my contract and salary, declaring "we're going to pay you £375 a week". I don't know what he expected my reaction to be but I told him I was earning a bit more per week at Crewe just being assistant manager but I tempered that by telling him that money wasn't a big issue for me.

To be fair to him he did say that although the club couldn't do much more on the salary front they might be able to top up the salary with crowd bonuses etc. I reiterated that the money wasn't a deal-breaker, I just wanted the opportunity to manage. At that point he virtually tore my arm off, stating "then that's yours" as he shoved a wad of A4 paper across the table at me. I looked at the pile, maybe 20 or 30 sheets thick, wondering what it was. "That's your contract. Read it and sign it," he added, beaming.

I looked at the contract, looked at him and said: "Look, just show me where you want my signature, take it away and send me a copy. You have a read of it, I'll have a read of it but basically, done deal, I'm coming. If you then have a problem with me, let me know. If I have a problem with you, I'll let you know and we'll address that situation as appropriate but I'm not sitting here reading through that."

I was desperate to have a go at management. I played under managers, coached under managers and now wanted to have a go on my own. I wanted to manage a football club, make decisions, create a team and basically wanted my own crack at creating a culture. I had experienced what I wanted to create, at Crewe under Dario, and it was time for the next chapter of my football life which began with being part of the football culture at Everton, as a fan, immersed in the historic culture. I look at the culture being established at Stoke

City and turning the clock back to what I wanted as I took my first steps on the managerial ladder was a shot at creating a culture.

The common factor between those two clubs I mention is the time David Moyes and Tony Pulis have been accorded to create a culture. There are those who say you need some luck as well but I don't subscribe to that. I believe you create your own luck and people like those two who have carved out and created a culture haven't done it through luck. When they have needed the time to create their culture they have got the result or set of results to do so by making a difference. They made the difference by their decision-making as a manager or a coach. A manager has to effect something, initiate something, that's the responsibility of the job and all of those things were what I wanted to do, at my club under my charge. I wanted that responsibility.

I went into Wigan Athletic quite open-minded, fresh and realistic at the opportunity that lay before me. I was bursting with enthusiasm but looking back it was a club that appeared to have been purchased just to sell on. I had a good working relationship with Stephen Gage, until the day I got the sack, but a few months after my departure we were in touch and there wasn't any lost respect. He had been quite upfront when he appointed me, black and white about the financial position. I don't suppose he could have been anything but open as the club had been relegated the previous season and all the assets had been stripped and players sold. Though people who will recall Springfield Park may scratch their heads at the thought of anything worthwhile being there to be stripped because it was still very much a non-league ground. That's not to do any disservice to non-league grounds today many of which are vastly superior to Wigan's ground in 1993.

There was no money at the club so that severely restricted my search for players. Where I was going to recruit from was a constant problem though my time at Crewe helped gather a wealth of knowledge from all the players I had seen when scouting while Dario concentrated on the coaching. I watched a lot of reserve games, and lots of non-league games where we used to get our players from. I would also see a lot of young players. It was an allocation of my duties at Gresty Road for which I was truly grateful when I was Wigan manager. The players I had seen may not have been good enough for Crewe a couple of years earlier but might well do for Springfield Park.

As manager of Wigan I didn't have a target, I just wanted to focus on getting my teeth into the job and I must admit to an extent it was more a case of the job doing something for me rather than me doing something for Wigan. I wasn't aware of the expectations though they did arise in due course. The fans and people at the club wanted automatic promotion or via the play-offs. It wasn't until we were halfway through the season that expectation was modified. Promotion was a dream which deteriorated as rapidly as our league position. The more I looked at it and despite it being more of a struggle than I thought it would be I tried to remain positive and get something out of anything that occurred. Even if we lost a game by one goal I would look at the positivity of a performance while the fans digested the lost points.

Because of the constraints I operated under and the unrealistic expectations I would savour every crumb of comfort I could elicit from the job. I had to view finishing 19th as an achievement because there were times during that campaign when the outlook was particularly gloomy. But three wins and a draw from our last six games ensured a better perspective than being 21st and staring relegation in the face.

After the season finished I went to supporters' functions and genuinely believed we had achieved something, I had achieved something, but I was still getting stick. I brushed it off as part and parcel of a manager's lot and actually thought I wasn't doing a bad job considering the tools I had been given and we did have some young players coming through. I was trying to convince others to be optimistic though poor attendances wasn't any basis for optimism. Even my enthusiasm and positivity was under attack, leaving me to wonder how I was going to turn things around.

It was quite busy that close season as I tried to recruit new players and I brought some in I thought would have a decent sell-on value. On the football front we were prepared as well as I could make us but as early as a pre-season friendly in Scotland the signs were not good. We went up for a weekend to play just the one game, against Hamilton Academical, and were hammered so confidence was low going into the opening league fixture just a week later. We lost 2-1 at Carlisle, the first of five consecutive defeats, though we did win both legs against Crewe in the Coca-Cola Cup for a 4-2 aggregate win which was a fillip and a feather in my cap to beat a team from the division above us. Then you knew the football fates were having a laugh when we drew Villa in the next round, despite a big payday.

I couldn't dwell on fiscal thoughts too long because I was too busy.

In between our fixtures I was driving all over the country trying to source players. I had one lined up from Wolves and another youngster from Everton who was available on loan and I needed to see both of them in action the week leading up to the Villa tie as well as trying to fit in a trip to see a Sheffield Wednesday player I liked the look of.

I shot over to watch Everton play in the morning before driving over to Yorkshire for an afternoon game because the Sheffield Wednesday player I liked was playing against Nottingham Forest who would also field someone I was interested in. I could then drive down to Wolverhampton for a 7pm kick-off. That kind of day was not unusual.

In my first pre-season as Wigan manager the major concern was inheriting a squad that numbered just nine players so I had to trawl around non-league for players from clubs like Nantwich Town and Northwich Victoria. My old friend Duncan McKenzie was co-opted on to the board then so he would keep me appraised of what was going on which is exactly what he did especially as that second season started so badly, which is why he kept pushing for me to make a signing. Little did I know how things were stacking up against me as I zig-zagged across the country trying to improve a team I would soon not be responsible for.

I managed to secure the Wolves player and that evening around 10pm Duncan rang me for an update. When I told him the lad was coming to Wigan he said "thank f*** for that". When I got home at 11.30pm I felt quite chuffed until I got a phone call from the player's father to say the lad wasn't coming to Wigan after all. He gave me chapter and verse but the upshot was despite his dad advising him it would be a good move and better to be playing league football at Wigan than reserve football at Wolves it seemed the lad's girlfriend had the casting vote. One major factor was the intervention of another club, closer to home, that very night.

So, after another driving marathon the rug was well and truly pulled, leaving me with a dilemma. Should I phone the chairman, having phoned him earlier to say the player was coming, just to give him a taste of a day in the life or leave it? I chose the latter. I will never know if what happened next would have been averted had I told him that night. I only know what did happen.

At 8.30am the next day Stephen Gage phoned me asking if I was all set for the player's arrival. I told him the bad news and explained why I hadn't called him the night before to tell him. Then he asked "what's going on here" so I told him and finished with something like "that's the way it is". "What do you mean that's the way it is?" he asked with increased dissatisfaction in his tone. I told him "these things do happen. All sorts of personal reasons can be the cause of a deal not happening". Then he got personal and asked if it was down to me. I asked what he meant and he became evasive with generalisations as he obviously realised he was blaming the u-turn on me. I responded by telling him it wasn't me and that it was more likely to be that the lad just didn't fancy Wigan, full stop. He was used to Wolves with all that club could offer and he probably, and "don't take it personally", didn't want to swap that for Springfield Park.

Then the mood of the conversation nosedived when Stephen said: "I just don't know where we're going, lately." My ears pricked up and I went on the offensive asking what he meant so he added: "Well I just don't know what the policy is or what your policy is." Then I had to let rip. "I'll tell you what my f****** policy is. If I can get someone for 20 grand you have a heart attack. If I can get someone on a free transfer you do cartwheels. That's the policy." He then asked what I was talking about and he just wanted to know where we were going before notching up the angst several stages to accusatory level.

"You're running around the country like a headless chicken, here, there and everywhere. You were out all day yesterday. You just don't seem to be here." I pointed out to Mr Gage that he had just described a normal day at work for his manager and repeated in a little less detail what I had outlined to him previously. His response was: "I just think we don't know what we're doing. In fact I think we'll have to chat when you get in."

The writing was now well and truly on the wall so I knew what to expect when I got to the ground. I went straight to his office and sat there while he outlined what had gone wrong, when it had gone wrong etc, etc. The list included reference to the previous day "when we need a signing we can't get one" and he covered just about everything possible before the *coup de grace*.

"I think we should just call it a day." When I asked him to be more specific he simply exhaled and said: "That's it." "So you're telling me I'm sacked, finished?" "Yes, in a way." So it came to pass, my first experience in a 20-year career in football of the single irrevocable fact in the game, for a manager, the sack. I gathered my belongings in a cardboard box and drove away from Springfield Park wondering why on earth I had not signed the one-year contract when I had the chance. It was a long drive during which I wondered what lay ahead. Then I heard what Duncan McKenzie did when he learned of my fate. He told Stephen Gage he was leaving too, adding he could stick the job "where it's pretty dark".

Shortly afterwards I spoke to Graham Taylor, more to inform him that his player had changed his mind than anything else, and Graham told me to make sure I was paid up by Wigan, which to be fair to Stephen Gage did happen. Graham said he would get his chief scout Bobby Downes to call me and arrange some scouting for Wolves.

That kept me ticking over in terms of staying on the football circuit although it was expenses only. I knew I could manage on my three-months severance pay-out, for three months at least, which would take me up to around Christmas. I tried to pick up other work but I rapidly discovered it can be very difficult with far more people seeking jobs in football than there are jobs available.

It was during the first couple of months of the New Year I received a call from Brian Laws. It was out of the blue as was his question "would you be interested in coming to Grimsby?" I was a little bemused as I had applied for the job as Grimsby manager. So I asked in what capacity he wanted me. He said assistant manager and first team coach because he had been interviewed for the manager's job and had been told by a couple of the directors he knew that the job was his, nice for me to find out I had been unsuccessful from someone I hardly knew.

It was a strange one so I outlined my reservations, namely that I didn't know him and he didn't know me and it wasn't how I operated. He said he had done his homework on me and spoken to Dario. He had also spoken to Frank Clark and Alan Hill at Nottingham Forest and, in Brian's words, "they recommended you". So when he asked me what I thought I suggested we met for a drink and a chat about what he expected and decide how we both felt.

We met as arranged and his opening was the need for a speedy decision from me as he would be pressured from the Grimsby end to have an assistant in place. He told me the position of assistant manager was even more crucial because he wanted to continue playing though he would make all managerial decisions. He said the bulk of the coaching would be down to me though he would do some as well. That seemed ok to me and then he said I would be earning around 35 grand a year.

I said the money was of no great concern to me as I was out of work. With what happened the following week I should perhaps have kept that particular comment to myself.

Brian said if I accepted the job he could tell the directors that same evening and it would see everything in place so they could arrange a press conference. I agreed to the offer and reported the following week but almost as soon as I turned up at Blundell Park Brian told me he couldn't give me what he had offered me in the first instance, namely the level of salary. He said the position and title was still there but the money was significantly less. He said there was nothing he could do about that but for me that was the first question mark about my situation with him almost before it got started. I told him it wasn't going to change anything and for me it didn't. I just got on with the job and it worked well with him playing and managing and me coaching. Results went well and the crowd seemed to take to what we were doing. We had a decent set of players though there was a shortage of talent and a lack of real pace but a good team spirit and consequently we started very well. Indeed by the end of November 1995 we were third though we did tail away to finish 17th but we spiralled downwards in the aftermath of the fall-out following the "chicken wings incident" between Brian Laws and Ivano Bonetti.

The first thing to hit me about the club was the dramatic improvement in players' ability when compared to that which I had known at Wigan. It was a much higher level and the standards of the division were much better and the football was better so that made it professionally enjoyable. The facilities weren't that good but it was a club that had sustained a decent level of football and a lot of that was down to the previous manager Alan Buckley. I felt I could influence Brian in those early months because of my experience and knowledge, because he was fairly new to it all. When we were looking for a new player I always seemed to be able to come up with a few suggestions, one of them being Tony Gallimore, brought in from Stoke City, who went on to make around 250 appearances for the Mariners.

Brian and I worked well as a team and we used to plan our scouting missions deciding who would go where and after each assignment we would touch base and report our findings to each other so we could formulate the next step. It was a professional relationship that was bearing fruit and, league position aside, it was running smoothly until Ivano Bonetti arrived.

Under normal circumstances a former Juventus player and European Cup finalist and Grimsby Town featuring in the same sentence would be the stuff of wild dreams. But that's exactly what happened with the arrival of Ivano Bonetti at Blundell Park just three years after he lost in the 1992 European Cup Final to Barcelona with Sampdoria. And from the very first to the very last there was nothing straightforward about the entire episode.

It was a revelation to even consider a player with clubs like the aforementioned on his CV, plus others, playing in the equivalent of the Championship for Grimsby. Maybe the attraction was the same black and white strip sported by Juve. Whatever his background I had never heard of him and neither had Brian but he came into the picture one night when I went to look at a young player at Aston Villa who was interesting a number of clubs at the lower levels. Because of that interest I felt he would be quickly snapped up so we needed to act fast. I knew he would improve what we had and I knew also that even though he might cost us a few quid importantly I also knew we could improve him and benefit further down the line.

At half-time during the game we watched I was sure we wouldn't get him because I knew Wycombe were looking for a left-sided player and from what I had seen in that first period from him I felt he would be beyond our means. As I came to that realisation I got talking with Gianni Paladini, who was an agent as well as being a restaurateur in Birmingham. He quickly got down to business and asked what I thought about his boy this evening. It seems that one of the centre-halves playing in the game was an Italian called Ivano Bonetti. Gianni was trying to get him a club in England and he was on trial at Villa. He asked what we were looking for so I explained and Gianni pointed to the long-haired centre-back and inquired "what about him?" When he named the player I said I had never heard of him. So Gianni reeled off a list of top Italian clubs, adding he was also a former Italian Under-21 international. He was then 31. I told Brian, who was with me that night, and he was hooked before I had got to the end of the list of clubs Ivano was credited with. He told me to "get him in and play him in the reserves this week".

All the necessary paperwork was processed and Brian, who was very media savvy, put out loads of publicity, which I guess was a bit of a novelty in our part of the world. Next thing I knew it was splashed across the back of the *Grimsby Telegraph* in banner headlines that we would be fielding a top Italian international in the reserves the following evening.

It certainly worked because the attendance for the reserve fixture was nearly as high as for a first team game, around 4,000 fans. They weren't disappointed because he looked different class. He was sharp and possessed of a sweet left foot, quick feet and a short stride. He could throw people off balance and get shots off from all angles and distances. Although Brian could see the football side of things he was salivating at the publicity factor; all I could see was what a difference Ivano would make to the team. Although he had a cavalier attitude I was enthused by something that seemed beyond our wildest dreams. We were hooked, all of us, and I left all the negotiations with Brian while I eagerly anticipated the best use of such a talent within the team. I wasn't privy to any of the details though I did get a first sniff of something that was commonplace in Europe but almost unknown in England, the enigma that was image rights. I don't know what kind of deal was struck to secure Ivano but I do know that negotiations did continue for some time as he was playing. There was a basic salary but I knew he was trying to negotiate a percentage of money through the turnstiles above a certain figure and a cut of shirt sales and suchlike. Those things were alien to me and went against the grain and were contrary to what I was used to in the domestic game.

Grimsby were 12th in the table when Ivano made his debut in a 1-0 win at Charlton. By November when he became a legend by scoring the only goal against visiting West Brom, managed by Alan Buckley, we had climbed to seventh. Ivano and Grimsby ended the month on a real high when his goal beat Tranmere away and took us third. They were heady times but from that point onwards we nosedived down the table, going nine games without a win. Ironically the ninth game before the catalyst that was the game at Luton Ivano's goal earned us a home draw with Derby, who were heading for the Premier League.

Although team spirit is integral to the efficiency of a squad I have to say that Ivano was a special case. He wasn't a big-headed fancy-Dan, he was just a very special player. He was accepted by the players and was very popular, he was certainly popular with the ladies. I got on very well with him and, on reflection, perhaps that didn't help with the friction that existed between him and Brian. He was a class apart and had a panache that was rare but I always felt there was a clash of personalities where he and Brian were concerned. Quite a lot of the ire between them was down to money and no short measure of ego. In truth it was there from day one but over the course of Ivano's stay at the club it simmered and grew until it boiled over as our winless run continued with a pivotal game at Luton. It wasn't just ego and money that was at the core of the unease between Brian Laws and Ivano Bonettii, there were other issues that contributed to the mix but it blew up after we lost 3-2 at Kenilworth Road just before St Valentine's Day. It became known at the "chicken wings incident" but it wasn't a plate of poultry that broke Ivano's jaw, made a mess of his movie-star looks and brought with it the kind of publicity Brian did not have in mind when we signed the player.

We had been doing quite well during the game and were leading 2-1 with 20 minutes left and had the win in our grasp but it went belly-up and we went 3-2 down. Brian was playing and from the far side of the field he was waving frantically to me. Lip reading, I could see he was saying "get that number 11 off (Ivano), get him off". I dug through the numbers and carried out the manager's instructions and off came Bonetti. As he crossed the white line he threw his gloves down in front of the bench but quickly retrieved them and was even quicker to apologise, saying to me he never intended any affront. "I wasn't throwing the gloves at you Kenny, I've just had enough," he said as he sat down to watch the rest of the game. At the whistle the team trooped off, heads bowed, and made their way into the dressing room. I went on to the pitch and saw Brian standing there, hands on hips, shaking his head. As I approached he said something like "I've had enough of him". I told Brian to let me handle this one, adding "you just count to ten".

I don't know whether Brian chose to ignore our normal protocol or just didn't care but he was so incensed he stormed into the dressing room. Ivano was seated having a sandwich or something and they must have made eye contact and that was it, blue touchpaper ignited. Ivano stood up and said something in Italian which, it transpired, translated to "are you trying to blame me for another defeat?" Brian flew across the room and hit him. Players jumped up and pulled them apart although it was more a case of pulling Brian off because Ivano was spark out. It wasn't a pleasant experience for anyone, it was bedlam. We obviously tried to keep things quiet in our dressing room and tried not to alarm anyone but that proved difficult as we were calling for a doctor. Eventually our physio went looking for a doctor but by then people had heard something was going on and really you can't hide that sort of thing for long.

It was an incident that changed things in many respects. Naturally it changed the relationship between Brian and Ivano. It certainly changed my relationship with Brian as it did between him and the other players. It also had a massive effect on the club and its reputation and was very divisive, making it difficult to claw anything back. It was a catalyst for everyone concerned.

What happened may have occurred in a football environment but it went way beyond. You are talking about moral responsibility and behaviour, what is acceptable and what isn't. But the upshot of the whole affair was its terminal effect on our season and although we eventually broke our winless streak, at the 15th attempt in trouncing Wolves 3-0, Grimsby finished just four points above relegation. You do get terminal incidents in football, take the Tevez row last year. I think they did well to contain that with all the innuendo flying around then. So it was in the wake of that night at Luton, a team we had thrashed 7-1 in the FA Cup. But within 15 minutes of the "chicken wings" flying everything had settled down and Ivano was being treated by the doctor. Brian and I went for a bath after everyone else had gone.

He knew what he had done was out of order. He turned to me, head in hands, and said: "Well, that's it, isn't it. I've had it. You can't do what I did." I didn't really know what to say then he added: "What can I do?" I told him there wasn't really a lot he could do other than get home to his family and have a good think. He repeated that he shouldn't have done it. All I could do was concur.

There was an air of expectancy around and everyone seemed to be waiting for some kind of action to be taken. Fortunately we had a game coming up very soon afterwards and the focus was necessarily on that. It wasn't just a case of putting it on the back burner to concentrate on the next fixture though some may have regarded it as such. I'm not sure Ivano was satisfied with what came his way in terms of an apology or club action. What the club did do was stage a handshake between the two of them, before a game. It was a token and there was great reluctance from both parties as they went through with it but you could sense from all concerned that it was just a gesture designed to get everyone back on track. Unfortunately those things are sometimes bigger than the game and need to be dealt with.

Most of us would like to think those things would not happen but they do and they have to be handled. Referring again to the Tevez episode when he faced the prospect of a worldwide ban even Harry Redknapp talked about the implications to the player's value when all of football knew that if he left City there would be some club somewhere that would take him. And such a club would almost certainly turn around and refuse to pay the asking price because of the potential for disruption. So the kind of incidents I am referring to have all sorts of repercussions, in the case of Bonetti versus Laws those repercussions impacted on me.

In the aftermath I found it difficult to work but I had the mindset that I should just get on with my job. It concerned the manager, the player, the club and all sorts of people but not me. My job, as assistant manager, was to assist the manager. My job as first team coach was to coach the players, but post- "chicken wings" it was difficult. Brian rang me the following day and the gist of what he said was he was "going to tough it out" which was quite a turnaround from his disconsolate stance in the immediate aftermath. He did just that but the strain on professional working relationships took its toll at the club as we battled to avoid relegation.

Early the following season I got a phone call from Keith Blunt at the National School, Lilleshall, where I had been doing some coaching while at Grimsby. He asked if I would be interested in a job in Sweden, at Malmo. I said yes and went over for an interview. They never offered me the job but were very professional and courteous in the way they conducted the entire process. I thanked them for the experience and returned to the reality of Grimsby Town.

It was a Blundell Park minus Ivano Bonetti, who left at the end of the season, but there was a carry-over when the next campaign began and a run of six games without a win at the end of the season continued with a poor start to 1996/97 when we lost three out of four games to sit 22nd in the table. The players who had been with the club at the time of the incident were obviously still affected and the knock-on was clearly evident on the park.

Brian managed to keep his job as our position in the league improved to 16th with a win over QPR but it proved a false dawn and we slipped back down with two draws and a couple of defeats before the final straw for the manager, a 3-0 home defeat to rock bottom Oldham Athletic. That was on the Wednesday night and on my way into the ground on Friday I heard the news Brian had been sacked. When I got to the ground I wondered about the implications for me and when I was with Brian, as he was clearing his desk, he informed me the chairman had said they were going to offer the position to youth team coach John Cockerill, who was a bit of a local legend. I asked him if the chairman had said anything about me and was a bit concerned when Brian said "no, we didn't discuss you". So I left him to pack up his worldly goods and decided I had better go downstairs and report in to the new boss.

John confirmed his new position and added "this is a monster task" to which I nodded. He went on to say he had grave doubts there would be any money to buy players and that they were only going to increase his salary slightly and that Brian was "earning double that". I thought to myself in those situations people's thoughts automatically turn to money while I was thinking "what an opportunity for him". Naturally I asked where it left me and he said I was still assistant so "let's see how it goes". John seemed happy with that though I told him to inform me if he thought that didn't work out. We got on with the first training session but then the next day when we came in the first thing John told me was that he was turning the job down, mainly because the club were only offering him a slight salary increase. I pointed out what a great opportunity it was, a first step on the managerial ladder but all he could say was that he felt we needed a quarter of a million pounds, maybe £400,000 to survive. I said he had to realise "this was Grimsby Town not Sheffield United" but it was no good, he had made up his mind and while I was wondering what would happen next John told me the chairman wanted to speak to me about the job. Cheers John!

I went to see the chairman that morning and he went through all that had occurred in the previous 48 hours, details I already knew. He confirmed Brian had gone although he gave me a different version of John declining the job, saying he didn't feel capable of taking the job at this stage. The chairman asked me to take the team for the next game and assume managerial responsibility. He said it would be on the same basis as they had offered John, until such time as a new manager could be appointed. That didn't matter to me, that was my chance although I hadn't thought it would come in the way it did but as the opportunity presented itself I thought I should grab it. My remit was to concentrate on each game as it came and that was how it was for a few weeks.

We lost my first game at home to Sheffield United, drew with Stoke and lost at Huddersfield so one point from a possible nine was hardly the stuff of legend so with a trip to Charlton coming up I was desperate for a result, a win that would make things look a bit better. I didn't often turn to Dario Gradi after leaving Crewe but desperate measures were called for so I rang him and as soon as he answered I said "HELP". I explained the circumstances and how limited my playing options were.

We did have some good players including Clive Mendonca who was a proven goalscorer but we couldn't keep the ball. I told Dario I wanted to make changes but couldn't. Dario asked if I had any kids. I told him Jack Lester was already in there and there was another I thought highly of, John Oster. Dario asked what he was like and I said I had liked him for a while but I was concerned he was a bit lightweight. He was a wonderful technician but he seemed to lack real drive and competitive spirit. He would suck a player in and then, boom, he was gone in a flash. Dario asked if he could play on the wing and when I told him John had pace to burn he said: "Play him on the wing then. If he's as good as you say he'll do ok. You're not in a good position and the chances are that you are going to go down and if you are going to go down at least give the kids a chance. Then people will say 'he never stuck with the old guard, at least he tried something different, at least he gave the kids a shot'."

So I decided to drop Craig Shakespeare and bring John Oster in. Craig was just coming back from injury but when I told him he took it very well and accepted a place on the bench when offered it. I asked him not to tell John and I never told John until we were ten minutes away from the ground. We beat Charlton 2-0 and although John never scored he was on fire that night.

That episode and the desperation for a result was brought home to me by the lead-up to that game, the pressure of wanting to do something but not really being able to so do. I was so grateful to the guidance Dario gave me because the pressure of expectation can be so intense. It's never ending, as a manager, and you have to develop a thick skin and even then you're not impervious to it, even if you're Alex Ferguson. I have always had a problem dealing with pressure and I think a lot of people think they can be a manager but the major difficulty is dealing with the pressure, in all its manifestations. But after that win and the justification for including John Oster and him coming up with a match-winning performance, it made the dressing room afterwards a joyous place, especially for the manager. Positivity was oozing from everyone, players, staff, even the media talked about an uplift and all the stresses and strains disappeared amidst that upsurge in positivity. The feeling didn't last long.

There was no money at the club, no back-up, no commitment and I was up against it from the outset. Never the less John Oster had made his mark and it wasn't long before the club received a bid of £1m for him. I told the chairman about John months before, when Brian was manager.

Brian would travel to Grimsby on match day but I would stay over and was able to watch the kids on a Saturday morning. The chairman would often join me at those games and one day I turned to him and asked if he could spot a million-pound player. He did a double take at my question and replied "for us?" I nodded and he was a bit flummoxed as he pointed to another youngster who was starting to attract attention. I told him it wasn't that lad but confirmed that he was going to be a decent player. Eventually the chairman picked John Oster out and that's when I told him that John could be a million-pound player. I was confident with that prediction because John was as good as I had seen at that level. Peter Reid, who was Sunderland manager at the time, had already bid £500,000 so when the chairman asked me what I thought I said we should get John on a contract for two years, which we did.

I told the chairman that all being well the following year we could get 30 or 40 games out of him meaning he would have the best part of 100 games under his belt before the end of his contract and still be the right side of 20 so goodness only knows what he would be worth by then. Before any of us got the chance to find out I got the sack and they sold him to Everton for nearly £1m.

I actually saw John shortly after that and while he wasn't maltreated he went the way a lot of youngsters did, being mismanaged. He was a first team player at 18 but after training in the morning he would drift away afterwards and had too much too soon and, not being handled properly, went awry somewhat. That's something that doesn't happen at Manchester United even with all the money there and at clubs like that but at that time it happened to him. At the right clubs with the right culture what happened to John does not happen although it isn't really down to the clubs, it's down to the manager and the culture established at a club.

It was only a few years ago the realisation hit me that football wasn't really about coaching, it's about the culture and the environment you create that leads to success. That culture is everything from the manager to the punters, it's all-embracing and culture is different everywhere. England went to play in a tournament in the Algarve a few years ago and at the end of a game against Spain there was a bit of a tussle, no more than handbags at six paces, and I thought nothing of it. Later that evening in the dining room I was walking past the table where some of the French coaching staff were seated and one of them asked me if I had a minute for a quick chat.

I sat down and everything was quite cordial and this chap asked me why we English "fight so much and how do you teach your players to fight as they do". I was a little taken aback and there was obviously a communication problem so I mimicked a few imaginary jabs to ensure I was getting the gist of what he was saying but he countered by saying "no, no, not fighting like that". And while he was searching for the correct word I explained that he meant compete rather than fight. His eyes lit up because we were now both clear as to what he was asking and said "yes, compete, how do you teach your players to compete so well".

I said that we didn't actually teach them, quite the contrary, we try to take it out of them. "Sometimes they have too much and at times we have a problem coaching it out of them." At that he threw his arms up in typical Gallic fashion and muttered "mon Dieu, the English have a problem because they have too much competitive aggression". The rest of his group were looking at each other in disbelief that we had so much fight that we were trying to, as I heard from one of them, "throw it away".

I tried to point out the sublime technical skills of French footballers but the coach responded by saying that technical skills can be taught but what English players had naturally "cannot be taught" and he beat his fist against his chest, no explanation necessary. I told him that was our problem. Then I thought with over 50% of players here being foreign and the influx of foreign coaches and managers you would think that our game and the tempo would now be influenced by those factors so we would now be playing a continental game but we are not. We're still playing high tempo, "in yer face" with passion and that's why everyone around the world wants to see our football. No one wants to watch the Italian league like they did ten years ago. People don't want stop start walking football they want the head-to-head, box-to-box football you get over here and that's why Rupert Murdoch pumped his money into Sky.

It's because of the nature of our football and people underestimate our culture. I mean the people in this country who actually run football, who influence football, are the wealthy owners. But the culture of our football, the style, tempo and everything else is totally owned and influenced by the public. You only have to see when a television camera catches the crowd at a throw-in or a corner showing the passion, the anger, the frustration and the involvement, every emotion known to man and experienced by fans the length and breadth of this country. It's war-like, tribal in a way and that's why the tempo is like it is and that's why foreign players can't understand our football culture. It's something that is ingrained in British footballers from the time they start to walk. Because it is cultural it's the same at all levels of our domestic game. The skill level may vary but players who have grown up in these islands are ingrained with a football culture and a culture is what I wanted to establish as a manager but time ran out at Grimsby and we were relegated.

It was a close-run thing between us and Bradford City to avoid that last relegation place and that was decided on the penultimate Saturday. Bradford won at home to Charlton while we lost at West Brom. So City went into the final game on 45 points, ahead of Grimsby who were on 43. We needed to win and hope they lost. I told the players as I sent them out to face Southend to focus on winning and forget what may or may not be happening at Bradford. As their manager I was proud of the response as they produced a season's best 4-0 victory.

Relegated by just two points they might have been but our players went down in style. It wasn't long afterwards that I met with the chairman Bill Carr for my P45.

It was the lowest point in my career when I got the sack at Grimsby Town. I had made the commitment by moving the family over and enrolled my son in school. That leap of faith wasn't helped by a constant fight against relegation for the duration of my tenure as manager and the fact that we came so close to survival was little consolation. To be fair I had a lot of people on my side among the media and the club's supporters but deep down there wasn't any trust in the board at Grimsby emanating from the stance I took over Ivano Bonetti. Some might say I had it coming if I realised the writing was on the wall but went ahead and with hindsight that was probably the case but I had this urge inside driving me on and convinced myself I could do it. It proved false optimism and resulted in the lowest ebb of my working life and family life and unemployment. It was my second descent into that state, after Wigan, and I decided that couldn't be allowed to continue.

We took stock for a few weeks. I would take Tom to St James' School and they gave tremendous support. It was the only positive from the move. There we were holed up in a part of the country I was prepared to make our home and give it a real go. But within a matter of months I was out on my arse. We stayed on because the truth of the matter was we had no idea where to go but I had to do something and at that lowest point something happened and that something is why I love Sir Alex Ferguson. He provided such a morale booster and one which saved me, saved us, on so many fronts.

I was unemployed and although Grimsby were still paying me that was due to end so we decided we had to put our house on the market. I was licking my wounds and we thought it best to head back over to Cheshire. That made sense because it had been our base when I worked at Crewe and Wigan so while all that pragmatic stuff was our main focus THE call came out of the blue.

The one director at Grimsby I felt was with me and in whom I had trust came over one night to talk to me. He was obviously a bit embarrassed because despite his support for me he was outnumbered by the rest of the board. But he'd not come across to commiserate, he actually asked if I could get him an autographed shirt for his daughter who was a big Manchester United fan.

I had a few contacts at Old Trafford in part due to my signing of Michael Appleton on loan. Michael did really well for us and stayed two months and livened the team up, livened the place up and made a terrific contribution towards our relegation battle. Indeed he made such an impact I truly felt we would survive, but he wouldn't stay for the third month and it was in that month we lost the battle to stay up. To be fair to Michael he saw an opportunity back at United to maybe get on the bench for some first team games.

So the Grimsby director knowing of my links with United asked the favour. I rang Carrington and spoke with Sir Alex's PA, telling her why I wanted it. She explained because it was May there was no one around but suggested she could get Sir Alex to do something and to leave it with her. Half an hour later the phone rang and when Lily answered it she turned to me and whispered: "It's Alex Ferguson." We exchanged a few pleasantries which wasn't easy as I was still in shock at the call. I apologised about the shirt and he said it was no trouble and he would sort it out but added: "More to the point have they (Grimsby) sorted you out? You know people think I have the best job in the world, which I have and I love it. But it doesn't stop me, every day of my life, getting up and looking over my shoulder. When this sort of thing happens to people like you Kenny it makes me look over my shoulder even more. That's a shame and I hope things go ok but how would you like to do some scouting for us?"

I said that would be great and then he asked if I had "been on holiday yet" and when I said no he asked if I fancied going out to Malaysia for the Under-19 World Cup. He said that United had someone going to one host city, Johor Bahru, and he wanted me to go to Kuala Lumpur. He said he was going on holiday himself but had spoken with Les Kershaw (then United's chief scout) and Les would sort me out with all the details.

My brief was simple. Sir Alex just asked me to report on the best players, "anyone you think is good enough for Manchester United". Just like that. He said there would obviously be a fee and all the flights, transport and expenses will be sorted for me, the club would take care of everything and he would speak with me when he returned from holiday. It was like manna from heaven and gave me a warm feeling when I came off the phone. When you have a real morose spell and you get a lift like that it makes you want to stick your chest out and makes you feel you can tackle anything. There I was out of work and drifting and Alex Ferguson took the time and trouble to phone me, help me, and trusted me to carry out an important task for him. That's why I love him.

I was away for about 12 days and watched a number of games and noted one or two players. I don't know if United followed up on my recommendations but the whole experience was a real fillip for me. Although new and completely different to what I had known it was a task requiring me to stay focused and that helped because it reignited my appetite for the game. I certainly didn't think I had worked myself into an employment situation at United, I just wanted to feel I had done a good job and it might stand me in good stead. I did say to Sir Alex I was going to apply for jobs and he said I could put him down as a referee. I also had help from Graham Taylor, who I had never met, after I left Wigan and it's a measure of people like them that they went out of their way to help me, a jobbing ex-footballer trying to cut a living out of the game.

The experience from my work for United gave me a new skill set and a taste for the scouting and talent identification which became integral to my work with the Football Association. I always felt I had a decent grounding in that respect at Crewe and the type of players we recruited but undertaking that task for Manchester United certainly enhanced my appreciation and aptitude for that aspect of football. When I returned I started making calls and in that process Mick McGuire at the PFA told me about a job opportunity at the PFA and asked if I would be interested.

The job was PFA coach in charge of coaching awards carried out for young footballers as part of the education programme. It was in the North East and not too far away from where I was, Grimsby, so he was going to suggest me to Jimmy Armfield who had overall responsibility for coaching at the union.

Mick spoke with Jimmy and told me I would have to apply for the job and be interviewed but if I was interested I would be shortlisted. I applied, was interviewed and within a couple of days the job was mine. I breathed a sigh of relief but there was still one problem. I told them I was selling up in Grimsby and moving back to Cheshire. I thanked the PFA for the offer and was grateful because I wanted to get back into football but I would rather go back to Cheshire and be unemployed than be employed but stuck on Humberside. If they weren't comfortable with that it would be a case of thanks but no thanks. But I did tell them if they wanted me to give it a go it wasn't that much further for me to travel from Sandbach than it was from Grimsby. "Give it a go" was the message from the PFA so I became the PFA regional coach for the North East of England. I also told Jimmy Armfield I wanted to continue with my work at the National School but before I took up the new post I made myself a pledge. We bought a house in Sandbach and after nearly 30 years of moving around the country that was it. No more moving.

It took some getting used to after the coaching I had been doing to change into a job where I was basically an educator. It was strange to drive into Manchester, park outside an office and go in, have a cup of coffee, talk to the commercial department and lots of other minutiae. I was part of a team and I got stuck into the job and as a consequence started to feel life wasn't that bad. I settled into my new role, as well as continuing my work at the National School, and as time moved on into the New Year out of the blue came a phone call from Robin Russell at the Football Association telling me there was a job available, as technical director at Lilleshall, and applications were being invited. There were a lot of things in my favour, I felt. I understood how things operated there, I knew a lot of the parents, and, with the National School being closed down, I was aware of how anxious the parents were feeling in that last year.

I was enthused but had only been in the PFA job for seven months. Jimmy Armfield was all for it, however, and said he thought it would be a good opportunity for me. But I was still concerned, as I didn't want to be seen as a job-hopper and had never really been anywhere for less than three years.

I obviously knew the National School was closing in a year, so why would I want to take a position with that on the horizon, much as I would love to take it on? I had grown to love the whole ethos at Lilleshall despite initial reservations about the elitism of such an institution.

The role turned out to be technical director at the FA National School for one year followed by two years as regional coach for the Midlands. I went for an interview and it took no time at all for me to accept the job once offered it! Because Academies were just starting up at that time Alex Gibson, who was North West regional coach, was leaving the FA to go to Manchester City. Howard Wilkinson said it would suit the Football Association if I could take on the North West. I did that and was able to stay where we were living and keep Tom at his school. And that's how things remained for the next four years as North West regional director.

Chapter 9

The National School Lilleshall, Thomas Telford and Back to the FA

Howard Wilkinson's *Charter for Quality* effectively closed the National School at Lilleshall because Academies were going to be introduced at football clubs. It was a vision of Howard's and I went into my job there fully aware that was going to happen. I joined the FA in a role that was only going to last for a year to wind down the National School and the next two years as regional director for the North West of England.

The regional director role was primarily coach education, helping the coaches, through qualification and in-service, who would work within football club Academies, basically teaching the teachers to teach. It would also include working with international youth players from Under-16 to Under-20 where I was privileged to work alongside one of the many great teachers of the game within the FA, Dick Bate. Generally our brief was to allow the clubs to direct their own initiatives and allow them to handle their own policies and to help facilitate that.

Another part of the role was identifying talent and pre-Howard Wilkinson, it was through regional trials from which players were selected for the National School, Lilleshall, players of the calibre of Michael Owen, Wes Brown, Jermain Defoe, Sol Campbell and Joe Cole.

In later years of the National School (1983-1998) some clubs were a little more reluctant to lose their best players to the School for two years when they would rather have them at their own clubs where they could influence and mould them and benefit from them. To be fair to Howard, having come from the game, he probably had a sympathy for the clubs' position in wanting to develop their own players. It was certainly part of his vision as to how he saw Academies with the hope of improving both the standard and prospects for young English players.

At Lilleshall I would stand in for Keith Blunt for a couple of days whenever he was called away and really enjoyed it. I was working on my own with a bunch of youngsters who were a joy to work with because all they wanted to do was kick a ball around after school. Working with a group of enthusiastic and talented young footballers was fantastic and the thought constantly going around in my mind was trying to imagine how good they were going to be two or three years down the line, real joy.

I was so keen on the coaching there that I would drop most things to go down there for my coaching sessions. When I went to Grimsby Town I told Brian Laws I wanted to continue my links with Lilleshall and he was happy with that in the early years. I would drive from Grimsby to Shropshire just to do a single session of an hour or 90 minutes at Lilleshall but loved it and felt it was worth every hour spent on the motorway. Eventually that was to prove a good investment as far as my time was concerned because it did lead directly to working full-time for the Football Association.

I was familiar with the staff at Lilleshall and the way things worked at the National School so when the chance of being employed by the FA came around I didn't have to think twice. It's curious in a way because over the years I seem to have been inextricably linked with the governing body through people I have worked with or for, like Dario Gradi, Dave Sexton and Dave "Harry" Bassett who tried to sign me when he was at Watford. There were links with the old Surrey Coaches' Association, the late Ted Powell and Roy Hodgson as well as the coach who took me for my preliminary coaching badge, Bobby Houghton. Those links in some way may have led me to working for the Football Association.

It was after my employment was terminated by Grimsby that my part-time work became full-time. If I was disillusioned or bitter with football at any time of my life the lowest and bitterest time was post-Grimsby. When I did eventually leave the FA after four years that was nowhere near as bad as leaving Blundell Park, but it was still bad. I have every sympathy with anyone who has been unemployed because it can be soul-destroying. I was devastated after 20 years of well-paid employment but thought I had enough collateral in terms of experience and profile in football to get by but there are no guarantees in this industry. It can be very unforgiving and can give up on you quite easily so when I finished with the Football Association I tried to see it as another chapter in my life.

My next step was a spell in the education sector at one of the most respected schools in the country, just down the road from Lilleshall, Thomas Telford School. I had a fantastic time at Thomas Telford though I never realised at the time the value of my spell there but I guess that is probably the same for a lot of people, not realising the value of something until much later, on reflection. What I did find was the awesome responsibility I mentioned earlier in this book, which I became aware of at Shoreditch when I was first dipping my toes in the education pool, suddenly became even more integral to my environment. My time at Thomas Telford also underpinned what I had encountered at college and what was reinforced during my career as a professional footballer and that is the togetherness, the camaraderie, or *esprit de corps* of sport.

I was by some way clearly the oldest member of the physical education department but was still fit and active so my age was no hindrance. Being around younger staff, and the children as well, rejuvenated me and once I got past the first six months I was in an entirely better situation than previously. After Easter the school football season wound down and the weather improved but suddenly I was gripped with trepidation as I realised the comfort zone afforded by football was soon going to be behind me and there was the prospect of what I was going to teach because the majority of what I had taught was football.

My anxiety abated somewhat as I thought I would just do a bit of tennis, a bit of hockey. I could throw a discus so athletics wouldn't be much of a problem. Then I thought about it more deeply and while I was ok with basics I didn't really understand the techniques required so I started going on all kinds of courses to improve my knowledge in those areas of sports which were basically new to me. Things like how to throw a javelin, properly, or how to execute a baton change in a relay etc, and the same for tennis and the other sports. But putting a positive spin on it I was having to stretch myself and make my discomfort more of a comfort, which I thoroughly enjoyed, and the flashback to Shoreditch and a similar learning scenario wasn't lost on me either. And I like to think had I gone into teaching on leaving college I would have been able to retain my enthusiasm, an enthusiasm which was given a kick-start at Thomas Telford.

Although I reflected a little on Shoreditch I did so to a much lesser extent on my football career. That was history and now was now, at Thomas Telford. My football career was gone, consigned to the memory bank of life. That was a previous life chapter and I was now writing a new one.

It was during that summer term, after I had been doing the two days a week for some time, that Sir Kevin Satchwell turned round and said "why on earth don't you come and join us full-time?" When I asked as what, quick as a flash he said: "Director of football, Thomas Telford's director of football." I said "you can't do that", but he replied: "I can, I'm the head." He added that he couldn't pay me what he wanted to but he would pay me within the pay scales as they were laid down. Kevin said it would be great for me and good for the school because he saw an expanded role, not just a job. He said I would not only be teaching the children but teaching them to teach, to coach. He talked about introducing coaching courses at the school which would be part of their vocational awards, something which many schools eventually did, so once again Kevin was an innovator. He saw it as an opening for the school and the pupils and by no means was he doing me a favour. It was typical of Kevin, captain of Shoreditch College FC, Sir Kevin Satchwell of Thomas Telford School, because he required a good work ethic from all his staff – and pupils for that matter. Top people are like that, Alan Sugar, Fergie, Kevin Satchwell, and there's me putting my mate alongside those people.

Kevin wasn't short on the advice front. He told me to "get some quality" into my life after all those years "running around like a headless chicken" in football at everyone's beck and call. When I said it was in my blood he simply said that was the one thing he couldn't understand about my industry. I know what he meant. He could comprehend how it could consume you day and night.

Being part of the physical education department I became aware of the insularity such departments generally have and because of that I believe PE departments can be huge driving forces in a school.

I experienced the team ethic at all my clubs, fortunately, and that was an extension of what I enjoyed at Ruffwood School. At Thomas Telford it was somewhat different because the PE teachers were presented with groups of children and part of the imparting of sport ability was the implementation of the team ethic. I am not sure if you can instil it but you can present it to pupils, by example and by the team values you stand for as a teacher and as an individual. That is a heavy responsibility because you have to be very aware of the example you are setting and of the values you are asking your charges to adopt. The wrong example can have irreversible consequences.

Much of the sport you find in schools is team oriented. Even sports that are very individual such as athletics are broken down from being a team, whether inter-house athletics or inter-school competition. There is a strength in a team sport, a team game and you have the expression whereby "the sum of the parts is greater than the whole". That sums it up perfectly, teaching that if a number of individuals give of their best in the team's cause it can generate a collective effort which seems greater than the sum total of the efforts of the individuals involved. That requires commitment to the cause and to refer once again to the Tevez affair, what he actually did was break the code and abdicate from that commitment, which is why the manager Roberto Mancini had such unilateral support for his stand.

When I started at the school I was pretty much thrown in at the deep end but it turned out to be a blessing in disguise. It slowly began to dawn on me when I had to pick up a mixed Year Eight group for hockey. I did know it was coming up so I had to plan for it and a new situation brought with it a new learning. It wasn't really a case of sink or swim and being told to get on with it and being given just a half-hour's notice. When you are trying to teach the game and the performance, it isn't just the techniques, because they are easy, it's applying them in situations where they have to produce that skill on demand and then in game mode. Then you had to talk about how a team performs when in possession and out of possession. Thankfully the principles were the same as football.

Kevin Satchwell was the other inspirational personality I encountered as an adult. Brian Clough inspired me as a person and as a footballer Kevin did likewise to the pupils entrusted to his care and that's exactly how he regarded his role. I watched him at my first induction evening, when he spoke to the parents of the new pupil intake. He addressed them with the hope and expectation of what the school was going to provide, what he was going to provide and what their children were coming to and what the school was going to do for them, the parents. It was basically a game plan for what the school was all about, its ethos, its philosophy and it made me bristle. It was brilliant and made the hairs on the back of my neck stand up because I was feeling part of that. Part of that process and part of that environment. He was positive and emphatic that every child would be treated as an individual and his or her best qualities would come to the fore. Kevin ended his speech with the promise to the parents that with their help the children would be prepared for the world they would live in and the school would maximise everything for them and give them every opportunity to make the best of the solid foundation they would get from Thomas Telford School.

Equally, he was just as sincere when he was seeing off the graduating class after they received their external examination results and were off to university, etc. He would shake hands with every one of them individually and wish them good luck. In the nicest possible way it was almost a case of, that's this lot sorted, onwards and upwards with the next year group to prepare and guide. He wasn't cold about it, it was the job and that was the duty, the responsibility. It was a duty of care. We were in the business of making kids into young adults ready for the real world.

And the same feeling is with me when I welcome the first group of young players with the England Under-16s. But something I learned from Kevin Satchwell was not to get too attached to a group of youngsters because you lose focus so I renew my enthusiasm for each group of young footballers, on an annual basis, to the point where I am about to hand them over to John Peacock and work with him at the next age level up. The symmetry with Thomas Telford continues because we want to take the England Youth players on to experience football at European level, if they're good enough. That's my job, and John's, to prepare them and facilitate them maximising their potential. And while that's going on I'm busy spinning the plates preparing for the next group stepping up to replace the ones who have moved up to the next level. It's as invigorating as it was in teaching but back in a football environment.

I have to regard the two years I spent teaching at Thomas Telford as a sabbatical although I never realised it at the time. It's only with hindsight I can see it was a point in my life when I needed what the school and teaching could provide. After two years I was feeling really settled and started to expand my horizons and began to put together a coaching school, after hours, whereby the students would be coached to level one award standard. So instead of leaving the school with ten GCSEs and two A Levels they would be leaving with ten GCSEs, two A Levels and a football coaching award. I was also working with girls' teams, which was new for me, and that was a challenge in itself, one I never relished to start with but one which I came to enjoy due to the feedback and response from participants who were new to the sport. It was very rewarding.

Looking back at what I experienced during my time at Thomas Telford and what I gained from it I was convinced at the time that was to be my career from there on in but just as I had reached that conclusion an opportunity presented itself to return to football and the Football Association.

There was an Under-18s match between England and the Rest of the World at Villa Park and the PFA were sponsoring all the transport and accommodation for the world squad. It was at that game I met with Sir Trevor Brooking, our now head of football development. He was in the early throes of his new role at the Football Association and he talked about the challenges he faced and the changes and opportunities that were unfolding as he set out his strategy for football development in England.

A part-time role emerged in talent identification, and shortly afterwards a coaching role with the foundation Under-16 squad. The combination of both roles and the responsibility that goes with them was too much to pass up. At the interview I was in the presence of not only Trevor Brooking, but also, ironically, the head of human resources, who had been present at my departure meeting following restructuring over two years earlier and was now welcoming me back!

Once the remit had been discussed I went back to Wolverhampton, where Kevin lives, that very evening. We had a couple of beers and he basically told me, with his full blessing: "You shouldn't have left in the first place. Get back and don't think twice."

There was only one potential obstacle, the period of notice, which in teaching is three months, so leaving at the time, July, didn't really give the school enough time to advertise for a post to start when the new term commenced in September. But, as always, Kevin saw opportunity not obstacle and turned to me, beer in hand, and said: "Looks like I could be teaching the first few weeks of the term. I could be the most expensive PE teacher in the country."

Back at the FA I was based at home in my new post and the set-up was very similar to how it had been previously. I could attend a meeting at one end of the country or be watching games, travelling abroad, it was still that varied. The only difference this time was the role being more expansive but more rewarding. As a national coach I was going to be coaching teams and players but as the role evolved with talent ID I became more involved in player development with Craig Simmons, who has been a tremendous font of experience for me over the last 20 years at Crewe, Lilleshall, and in my current role.

I now manage a network of regional scouts who meet regularly to formally report information. This information is recorded on our youth talent database by Jane Baker, who was instrumental in setting up this system more than ten years ago, and has worked closely with me to develop it further.

In many ways I have an ideal job which has more to it at the younger levels within the England set-up than coaching the players on the field. There is a great deal more off-the-field responsibility too because these young players are, after all, only with us for short periods of time. That can constrain effectiveness and one of the biggest difficulties we face has little to do with football.

Young international players are products of their generation and affected by all the influences upon them. I personally can't ever attribute any blame to a youngster with problems, they are who they are because of their upbringing and their environment. You don't choose your parents and you don't choose your way of life, you live that life. Parents nurture you or they don't nurture you. They give you standards or they don't give you standards. They give you disciplines or they don't give you disciplines. Children are a product of the environment they come from so for me, all we attempt to do with our lads is create an environment in which they can prosper and for their talents to come through. We aim to create a secure environment for them while they are with us. We are a temporary family, *in loco parentis*, and that is something emphasised to our staff as well as the youngsters. Our duty for that spell of time is to look after them. We don't impose harsh restrictions on youngsters who come to us, we actively encourage them to develop naturally and form their own codes of behaviour, conduct and values.

My job is invigorating. I don't wake up in the morning, ever, and moan about having this, that and the other to do or I've got to drive somewhere or stay home and make 57 phone calls. If you can't enthuse young players you shouldn't be working with them. If you impart negativity you will find that youngsters are the most receptive beings in the world and will pick up on that too. They have receptors to security and insecurity and will know when they are wanted, when they are cared for and respected. They will know when they are valued or not valued and will pick up on any negativity so quickly. Kids are really sharp and underestimating that sharpness is something to avoid.

There is a constant evaluation of young players and the information gathered is not only garnered by us as we are in constant communication with the clubs. Clubs will offer their views on how they see their players developing and the extent to which those players are involved in various tournaments. Whoever is seeking or offering information and for whatever reasons there is one key common factor in the entire scenario and that is the player. It is the one factor that should be the prime consideration.

Clubs are now benefitting from the experience of European club competition and tours encompassing all ages but I still feel the injection of ambition gained by representing one's country can ignite appetite for young players. A game for England can be so magnificent for a lad with the knock-on positive effect for his family, friends and school.

The confidence that can ensue from playing for England can be immense. Regularly we get feedback from the clubs that is so positive. They say how much a certain player has kicked on since he went away to play for England. That's the power of opportunity, the right opportunity. It is an opportunity for an individual player with benefits all round. The youngster benefits by improving himself and his game. He goes back to his club brimming with confidence so they benefit and when he returns to play for England the country benefits in the long term.

Compromise may need to be the order of the day because when both interested parties air their views the heart of the dialogue and action taken must centre on the long-term interests of the player. That must be the focus.

The power and appeal of the Premier League globally has grown to levels I don't think anyone ever anticipated. It has mushroomed beyond expectation and clubs, big clubs, have worked extremely hard commercially in all corners of the globe and have made it such an appealing brand everywhere. There's not a bar or hotel, anywhere on the planet, where you cannot see Premier League football. You can always find a telly showing our top flight football. I remember a few years back when Chelsea were celebrating their centenary my son told me the club were planning a celebration match against Brazil at Stamford Bridge. Tom said: "That would be a good game wouldn't it?"

I was taken aback because I thought that WOULD be a bloody good game because despite the fact they are an English club they did have players from all round the globe, some of the very best from different countries. And they were going to be pitted against the best that only Brazil could choose – they would only be from that one nation whereas Chelsea could choose from the entire planet so what a game that would be.

That is how football has changed because the world has opened up so much and the financial muscle now available means that clubs can go and purchase players from anywhere in the world. And, of course, certain clubs can quite literally buy any player creating the situation where a club side can be greater than an international side, on paper at least. That's how the game has changed but what I hope will remain is the appeal or national identity of every country. World Cups will never go away despite the growth of club football but it was interesting that Fergie said not long ago that the Champions League is probably now bigger than the European Championship.

Not many would argue against that but I do hope that the international arena will remain attractive for players and the general public. I think it will because of the identity and tribal aspect of support for international teams but it also has to be recognised that we live in changing times. There has been a significant swing from international football to club football, in some countries. The fact that Manchester United or Chelsea could potentially give England a game is neither here nor there as far as I am concerned. I think years ago you could have argued, say during the last few years of the National School, that Manchester United's best two English players or Aston Villa's best English players were better off being there playing with the best in the country on a day to day basis because it was going to move their game on playing with and mixing best with the best. But that was then. Now the big clubs have got such an array of talent, and foreign talent as well, I couldn't stand up and support that notion even though I still believe we, England, have got some real talent.

Football has always been an industry but nowadays it has grown into such an international force that it has affected everything to do with the game. Not so many years ago there was a bit of friction between a major Premier League club and England over some issue and it ended in chants of "yer can stick yer f****** England up yer arse". I was shocked because all those people were obviously pledging their allegiance to the club and were basically saying "forget England, we aren't interested in England we are only interested in our football club".

It proved a bit of a watershed for me in terms of where football was heading, representative of the way the groundswell of opinion was, coming as it did from such a big club in the land and one with a massive global presence.

Chapter 10

The Final Chapter

By the time this book comes out I will have celebrated a significant birthday and should be in the middle of celebrations to mark the 30th anniversary of winning the European Cup with Aston Villa.

It has been quite an experience reflecting on a lifetime of football and despite the milestone birthday I truly hope there will be more to reflect on in the coming years but what has been a standout for me in recalling the past is what a fortunate life I have lived. I certainly achieved far more than I would have thought possible.

Coming late into professional football, certainly later than the vast majority of my contemporaries, was a bit of an advantage because I do feel the extra maturity stood me in good stead. Being that bit older meant I could enjoy it as an adventure rather than grow into it from an early age, as was usually the case for young professional footballers. They would grow up with it whereas I had to grow into it and starting in my early 20s I feel enabled me to remain relatively unaffected by mixing with star footballers I had watched as a teenager, though I did allow myself the occasional "wow" when playing against the likes of Alan Ball.

From a physical perspective, I couldn't have coped with the demands of professional football at 16 or 17. I was probably a classic late developer and almost certainly one of the most significant periods in my physical development occurred when I was at college and received a boost to my physique while working on the roads humping concrete kerbs around. While labouring, my future lay in teaching and it would have been beyond my wildest imagination to envisage being paid to play football beyond the few quid I managed with Wycombe. But that one small step with Wanderers started me off on a football – laden path which has given me some priceless experiences in the game from many different perspectives.

From being paid as a professional to play football I have been paid to manage, (not very well as the records show), been paid to coach and paid to watch and yet still I regard it as a hobby more than a job. I feel I have been in a privileged position most of my working life and whilst there are tangible reminders in terms of winners' medals and trophies there are a million or more memories.

I remember sitting at Wembley watching Barcelona versus Manchester United and, as the game unfolded, thinking if United win this or get something out of this it will be a truly outstanding achievement. I think, going into the game, Barcelona were on a slight dip while I felt United were on a bit of a rise. I think Barcelona are probably the best club side I have ever seen and looking back on all the plaudits heaped on them in the wake of their victory over United I don't think I am far out in thinking there is also a certain humility about them. I remember when the players were tossing Pep Guardiola up in the air afterwards and the camera caught all their faces looking upwards as they tossed him skywards and it almost looked as if they were looking to the heavens and praising the Lord. There was shared joy, gratitude and respect and, dare I say it, love. It's their culture.

Messi does it for the love of football. It's not about the money for him. He loves his football and is the ultimate team player. I'm not referring to his goals but the fact he can be relied upon. Putting his foot in, tracking back and chasing all over the place to do a proper job as a professional footballer. Everyone talks about Barcelona in possession of the ball but, my goodness, look at what they do when they don't have it. Take the ball away from them and see what happens when the opposition have it, the Barca players go after it with a vengeance. They hunt in packs and in terms of pressing, not just in ones and twos but as a unit, they are an absolute joy and a masterclass to learn from in terms of their appetite and work rate. The intensity of their application is an education. They are a team, a squad, a philosophy that's emerged over the past few years. You might have a team that is good with the ball or you might have a team that is good without it but to have a team as excellent as Barcelona are in both aspects of the game is rare. They are so good, I get so excited they get me off my seat. It's the same when I watch kids who can do that and in this country we do have a lot of young talent despite what some doom and gloom merchants write in the media.

I know in my business when you are trying to develop players you have to be aware it is a results-driven industry and there is huge kudos in delivering results but I do get a massive kick out of watching good players irrespective of whether we win or lose. Maybe I shouldn't be saying that but as I am in the business of player development I can be forgiven. I marvel sometimes at some of the things young players can do and at the top end of the game what Barcelona can do, in possession of the ball. But the thing that really impresses me is that other side of the game which, sadly, our best players probably lack.

Our very, very best players, in possession, are as good as anyone in Europe but that other side of the game; winning the ball back and how to be effective when out of possession, that is where there is room for improvement.

It's impossible to overstate how important psychology is in sport, not just football. It's the biggest influence. I think games are won and lost, and success is based, on fear and belief, how much fear you have in you and how much belief. If you've got a little fear and lots of belief, you've got a chance. If you have a lot of fear and a little belief you've got no chance.

A few years back our Under-17s were in Belgium for the Uefa tournament which we lost, in the final, 1-0 to Spain. Chelsea had invited all their European scouts to our hotel for a meeting with Frank Arnesen, who was the sporting director at Stamford Bridge and afterwards they were going to watch Chelsea play, at Anfield, in the European Cup semi-final on TV.

My son Stephen was on the phone to me asking me how I thought the semi-final would go and I told him I thought Liverpool would win. He wasn't satisfied with that, pointing out that Chelsea were playing well going into the game but I was sure. I was so sure because as the build-up got ever closer to kick-off I had watched the warm-up then the players coming out and the Chelsea staff on the bench. And there was just something about the way the Liverpool players took to the field and the look in their eyes and the way their body language exuded belief.

Frank Arnesen was sitting near me and I turned to him and attracted his attention and asked him how his English was. He said "fine" so I said he would understand the word "fear". He nodded and said: "That's when you are worried." I then asked if he understood the word "belief", and he nodded and said: "That's when you have faith in things and believe them to be true." So I told him this game is all about fear and belief and your manager and your bench and your players are showing all the signs of fear and there's a tidal wave of belief out there. You can't see it but it's there in the body language and you can feel the expectation of that fortress they call Anfield, and it killed me to say that, being an Evertonian. Chelsea heads were hangdog, necks were disappearing into shoulders and they weren't just up against 11 red shirts – they were up against an army, an incessant, merciless belief and a tradition. I remember looking at Jose Mourinho, who almost looked as if he was wondering what it must be like to have that behind your team.

Every dressing room I have been part of has been good, with good people, good footballers. There was camaraderie and companionship, loyalty, trust, solidarity and ambition. All those things exist in every dressing room. It's a family and like in any family there are tensions, rows and upsets but it's the culture of a club that decides how much any negativity affects what happens on the field. The better and stronger the culture the more it reduces adverse effects. If a culture is not strong enough any of the upsets which can beset a club can destroy what a team tries to do on the pitch.

There are many factors that contribute to a team on the field of play and one of the regular chestnuts that crops up whenever football is discussed, usually in the wake of an England international, is "systems". We've got 4-3-3, 4-4-2, 3-4-3, and Christmas trees etc etc and I have come to a conclusion. I can't really call it baloney but I think those days are gone. I think the important things in football to implement and apply now are the old-fashioned principles of the game, from the day when all we had was Walter Winterbottom's WM formation. Those old-fashioned principles are simple and will never change.

The reasons why teams win football matches and the reasons why teams lose football matches are usually based upon principles, not systems. If a team wants to be successful and win things they have to threaten the goal. That duty or responsibility doesn't fall on the shoulders of a striker alone or your strike pair or two wingers – that burden falls on the whole team although the emphasis does seem to levy that responsibility on strikers but goal threat comes in all shapes and sizes and approaches. There are lots of players who don't really threaten the goal but are forwards. They may be able to run past people but they don't get many shots in so they don't threaten the goal. They don't pose defenders problems because they don't run in behind, they run across them or in front of them or keep the ball but maintain possession in front of defenders while not really threatening the goal. A team that never concedes a goal will never lose but a team that never scores a goal will never win.

Brian Clough, then, and Sir Alex now, are exponents of having goal-threatening players whether they be strikers or midfielders or from wide areas or from set-plays. Success is based on threatening the opposition goal unless it's a one-off cup game where the tactics or game situation might require otherwise. All successful teams have goals in them. As well as forwards who are goal threats they would have midfield players who might weigh in with five or six goals a season or defenders who might come up with three or four, as Villa had in 1981 and 1982.

As I've got older the game has become simpler for me to understand. When I was playing it always seemed a bit more complicated and when you heard some coaches talk they made it seem more complicated than it appeared. What has hardened for me is a belief that the game is fairly simple. I find it easier to understand why teams win games and why teams lose games and ultimately it is about winning and losing for most because that is the outcome of your labour and learning for that 90 minutes.

The basic principles of play in football will never change because it is an invasion game which requires keeping and regaining possession of the ball and scoring more than the other team to win. Putting the ball in the opposition net and keeping it out of yours was fundamentally what Brian Clough preached, and it didn't do his teams any harm. That is where I am at and what I coach is an understanding of the principles of play and their application. The task for all coaches is to teach and look for evidence in training or games that learning is taking place.

Now when I see some evidence, i.e. the decision making when attempting to put these principles into practice, then I think "he's got a chance, he's learning"! Teaching how to be effective in possession and how to be effective when without the ball is almost a case of trying to get over the state of mind many people have that you cannot affect the opposition when they have the ball. But you can.

That's where I get my enjoyment, now, coaching those basics of possession, retaining and regaining the ball. The general perception is football is only enjoyable if you have the ball but it is my contention that you can have pleasure without the ball and that is what I try to impart. I want coaches and youngsters alike to think being without the ball isn't just hard work.

Playing football is all about having fun and being paid as a professional to play is being paid to have enjoyment. I don't believe there's anyone out there playing football who is thinking 'what time am I going home?' because it is totally absorbing, all consuming. It has always been like that for me and even more so as a coach.

I started as a player in 1973 and played my last game in 1992. That was only one chapter in my life, a chapter that began with me being a forward and ended in 1992, as a defender. I am finding the game more absorbing as I now match 19 years of playing with 19 years of coaching. It is even more captivating and more enjoyable and I want young players to take pride in, and enjoy being rewarded for, the other side of the game, when not in possession of the football. I look at the career Jamie Carragher has had and think back to when he started at the National School, as a forward. He has gone on to be England's best defender, certainly in my time as a coach. Because I went through a similar rite of passage, playing the bulk of my career as a defender, I learnt late about the art of defending. It was a learning curve which continued into coaching and is still there. Though football without the ball may be perceived by some as less glamorous I have found the polar opposite. Defending is enjoyable and that is my perspective when it comes to working with England Youth players, so it is fitting to highlight Jamie Carragher who makes defending look so enjoyable too!

They say crossroads and new dawns occur whenever a new coach or manager takes up his new post but I can justifiably say whilst these events take place the hard work, patience and commitment of youth coaches at club and national level continues and we can all be optimistic with the depth of talent emerging over the past three or four seasons.